Praise for *How to Manage Your Home Without Losing Your Mind*

"*How to Manage Your Home Without Losing Your Mind* is the most entertaining home management book I have ever read. I told my husband, 'I can't believe I didn't fall asleep once while reading a book about *cleaning*!' Instead of overwhelming the reader with an extensive list of things to do, Dana humorously eliminates your guilt while providing simple, actionable steps that will make a profound impact on your home. Since I implemented Dana's strategies, my house is cleaner, more organized, and most importantly, more peaceful."

—ALEA MILHAM
AUTHOR, *PREP-AHEAD MEALS FROM SCRATCH*

"Although life was so overwhelming that the thought of reading this book exhausted me, I read it anyway, and something clicked. Cleaning once wasn't working for me. By doing the same small tasks every day, I'm finding that my house is getting cleaner and I'm hating the thought of housework less. While my house still has a long way to go, I'm thrilled with the progress I've seen and hopeful about the future!"

—LISA THOMPSON
BLOGGER, FUNHAPPYHOME.COM

"A hilarious, practical, yet brutally honest look at the way we manage and keep our homes. . . . Dana's way of deconstructing our fantasies about cleaning and organizing, followed by practical advice and wisdom, is why this book is a must-own for all those struggling to keep up with their homes. You'll be revisiting her words and tips over and over again."

—ERIN CHASE
AUTHOR, *THE $5 DINNER MOM COOKBOOK* SERIES,
AND MOM TO FOUR MESSY BOYS

"Let's face it: reading about cleaning and organizing is more fun than actually cleaning and organizing. I was fully prepared to read, enjoy, and promptly disregard Dana's book, but when I began reading, something weird happened. On page 10 I shut the book and cleaned my kitchen. . . . I later read more and made my way to page 80. I put the book down again and began tackling laundry. . . . Could a book actually spur a person to action? Could an author actually urge me to be a better homemaker and give me practical ways to make that happen? *Yes* and *yes*! I'm actually crying thinking about how Dana is such a blessing to me and to my family."

—AMANDA FROM INDEPENDENCE, MO
HOMESCHOOLING MOM OF SEVEN

"It's like Dana was writing this just for me! I can't tell you how many times I have searched for the right method that was going to solve all of my housekeeping woes, or been sure I would keep my house clean forever after a particularly deep cleaning of the house. . . . As someone whose room was once mistaken by police as having been ransacked (it wasn't), I need someone who understands what really makes me tick. In this book, as always, Dana is funny, helpful, and sometimes brutally honest. Thanks for keeping it real!"

—ANGIE KAUFFMAN
BLOGGER, REALLIFEATHOME.COM

"This is not like any other organizing book out there. Dana does an amazing job of helping a disorganized, junk-collecting procrastinator, like me, see that I really can get my clutter under control. She doesn't do it as a know-it-all organization guru but as someone who has been where I am and is in the trenches with me. If you're ready to retrain your brain and start the deslobification process (as Dana would put it), then this book is for you!"

—SARAH ROBINSON
BLOGGER, SIDETRACKEDSARAH.COM

"I love the approachable, compassionate, and fun way that Dana writes about universal struggles—like housework that is never done! I gleaned good tips (love the Container Rule and Do Easy Stuff First!) but I also gained a better understanding of those in my family I may have labeled as slobs along with how to approach them. (Hint: do not give them more stuff!)"

—JAMI BOYS
BLOGGER, ANOREGONCOTTAGE.COM

"There's so much in the book that's insightful, humorous, and time-tested. I especially like the term *procrasticlutter*. My house is full of it! This book has really helped us look objectively at each room, drawer, and shelf in our home. As I write this, the dishes are put away and my kitchen is clean. What a wonderful feeling and a great way to start my day."

—JANET DUNLAP
PROFESSIONAL HOUSE CLEANER, SOON-TO-BE EMPTY NESTER, AND MOM OF SIX

"I have read every bestselling book out there to help me get my house under control. I can identify the stuff in my home vs. the items that bring me joy. I've worked through how-to checklists and posted purging questions to help me make decisions wherever I've decluttered. And even though I found valuable tidbits in all of them, none gave me hope for a real change in my household—not until I read

How to Manage Your Home Without Losing Your Mind. The Container Concept hit me like a ton of bricks."

"Finally, an organizing book for those of us who need it! And it's written in a simple and hilarious way that our non-linear-thinking brains can understand and implement. . . . Dana leads you step-by-step with the heart of a woman who has been there and struggled with the same issues you are currently struggling with. Really, this is a must-read for anyone who wants to learn the secrets that all those organized types seem to know."

"Oh, Dana, have you been a fly on my wall? How refreshing to read this book and see myself in it, page after page. . . . *How to Manage Your Home Without Losing Your Mind* is full of funny, practical wisdom. If you need a remedy for your household woes, this is an easy pill to swallow, because it is laced with humor, real-life experiences, and true solutions. Dana's principles will motivate you and change your way of looking at your home. For once, you may just feel like you can get a grip on your home!"

"When I was asked to read a book about cleaning and decluttering, I was a bit hesitant. I felt like a failure already. Did I really need to read yet another book full of tips and tricks that would leave me feeling worse? From the first page, I was put at ease. It's okay just to do the dishes? Really? I didn't have the usual feeling that I needed to just fire bomb my house and start over. Instead, this book gave me hope! . . . The appendix alone is worth buying the book. I want to print it and glue it to my wall as a life map."

"I laughed my way to a truly clean(er) house! *How to Manage Your Home Without Losing Your Mind* doesn't just tout another organizational method that sparks inspiration and then fizzles. Dana White uncovers the reasons most organizational ploys fail and delivers real, practical, attainable hope! Adjusting my thinking to reality about managing my home has already set in motion sustainable change.

This is the first organization book that I have ever read that was written by someone who isn't naturally organized. And I loved it. No judgement, no superiority. Just a whole lot of real, practical help with a good dose of humor and hope."

—SHELBY FROM MONROE, WA
BUSINESS OWNER AND MOM OF FIVE

"This is the most helpful and entertaining book on housekeeping I've ever read! I loved getting cleaning advice from one slob to another. Dana's tips on decluttering were just what I needed to figure out how to declutter my own space. Living in a small apartment, I have found myself almost buried in stuff. I've already started simplifying my life using her strategies."

—PATRICIA FROM RENO, NV
HIGH SCHOOL MATH TEACHER AND PART-TIME GRADUATE STUDENT

"Praise the Lord, and pass the dishrag! Finally there's a book that speaks to a slob like me with commonsense approaches that make me think, 'Hey, maybe I *can* do this.' And all presented with a healthy dose of humor and humility. This book lays out the hard truths of a clean house but in a way that doesn't make me feel silly for not having embraced them before."

—EDITH FROM CLINTON, MS
CDO OF A NATIONAL BANK, MOM OF ONE, SUFFERS FROM SEVERE ANXIETY

"Even though this book was written for people who struggle managing their home, I found it applicable to people who struggle to get things done in general. If you are looking for no-nonsense, practical advice for overcoming *you*, you'll want to read this book. The house will never clean itself, but Dana's straightforward style will help you manage your home in a way you never thought possible. Forget fifteen-point checklists and chore charts—Dana cuts quickly to the core issues behind being a slob and helps you conquer them once and for all."

—TONI ANDERSON
BLOGGER, THEHAPPYHOUSEWIFE.COM

"Cleaning is the worst. But Dana White? She's the best! Especially when it comes to geting me to empty my dishwasher. This book is motivating and engaging but also easy to relate to, as Dana shares her own struggles openly. But my favorite part? The humor. Dana is laugh-out-loud funny, which makes me take what she says seriously. I might still hate cleaning, but I love this book and the way it's transforming my home."

—MARY CARVER
COAUTHOR, *CHOOSE JOY*

How to Manage
Your Home
Without
Losing Your Mind

How to Manage Your Home Without Losing Your Mind

Dealing with Your House's Dirty Little Secrets

Dana K. White

W PUBLISHING GROUP

AN IMPRINT OF THOMAS NELSON

Published in Nashville, Tennessee, by W Publishing, an imprint of Thomas Nelson.

Thomas Nelson titles may be purchased in bulk for educational, business, fund-raising, or sales promotional use. For information, please e-mail SpecialMarkets@ThomasNelson.com.

Any Internet addresses, phone numbers, or company or product information printed in this book are offered as a resource and are not intended in any way to be or to imply an endorsement by Thomas Nelson, nor does Thomas Nelson vouch for the existence, content, or services of these sites, phone numbers, companies, or products beyond the life of this book.

ISBN 978-0-7180-7995-6 (SC)

ISBN 978-0-7180-8323-6 (eBook)

Library of Congress Cataloging-in-Publication Data

Names: White, Dana, (Dana K.), author.
Title: How to manage your home without losing your mind : dealing with your
  houses dirty little secrets / Dana White.
Description: Nashville, Tennessee : W Publishing, [2016]
Identifiers: LCCN 2016008307| ISBN 9780718079956 (trade paper) | ISBN
  9780718083236 (eBook)
Subjects: LCSH: Housekeeping. | House cleaning.
Classification: LCC TX321 .W45 2016 | DDC 648/.5--dc23
LC record available at https://lccn.loc.gov/2016008307

Printed in the United States of America

HB 05.10.2023

To my husband, Bob. Thanks for embracing my special brand of crazy. Life with you is so much fun.

Contents

Part 1: Reality Check

Part 2: Daily Stuff: The Down-and-Dirty Truth About a Clean House

Contents

Part 3: Decluttering: The Down-and-Dirty Truth About All Your Stuff

Part 4: Change That Lasts

Who Needs This Book?

Dear Person Who Picked Up This Book (and is flipping through the first few pages, deciding if you should buy it),

Let me help you decide. Not everyone needs this book. Rule yourself out as my target audience if you buy home management books because you get a kick out of cleaning and organizing gives you a thrill. If your home is ready for unexpected guests more often than not, you probably don't need this book.

If you truly can't understand how someone could sleep while dirty dishes are in her sink, close it up right now and move on to something else.

Okay. Now that it's just us, I'll talk to those who *do* need this book.

If you sleep like a baby, unaware your kitchen counters are piled high with dirty dishes, but want to cry when you walk into a disastrous kitchen the next morning, keep reading.

If you've ever wished you could donate dirty clothes because you're so behind on laundry, you need this book.

If you're continually overwhelmed in your home, and you've failed to change your housekeeping ways so many times you just don't know if you have the energy to try again, this book is for you.

This is the book I never dreamed I'd write. If you'd told me six years ago I would one day write a book about cleaning and organizing, I would have laughed in your face.

Loudly.

And for a really long time.

After I caught my breath, I would have launched into a lengthy (and rather preachy) explanation of why I'd never do this. Using vague words like "struggle" and "personal challenges," I'd be clear that due to my own passion for authenticity, I would never write about this particular subject.

Because this particular subject made me feel like a failure. A complete failure.

Why would anyone write a book about the thing she struggles with most?

As a theatre teacher turned stay-at-home mom, I craved a creative outlet. I discovered blogging. When I realized moms were writing and other moms were reading what they were writing, I knew I had to have a blog. Actually, I was obsessed with the idea of starting a blog.

Obsession is my style.

But for a year and a half, I didn't. My house was a disaster. A continual disaster that magically reappeared no matter how hard I worked.

I'm not saying someone can't have a blog while her house is a wreck, but I couldn't. I knew myself and my history of messiness enough to know I couldn't let one more thing distract me from my house.

And I didn't want to be a fraud. I feared if I wrote rosy and wonderful things about motherhood and my passion for family, I'd be labeled a fraud if someone found out what my house looked like. I knew there was a disconnect, and I despised it.

Even with my new "I want to start a blog!" motivation for getting my house under control, I kept failing. In a moment of inspired desperation, I started a blog called *A Slob Comes Clean*. It was my completely anonymous practice blog, my way to justify blogging. I planned to use it as a place to learn about this fun thing I wanted to do, while keeping my focus on my house so I could finally get it under control.

I figured this experiment would take me three or four months. Tops.

I'm now pushing a decade of what I've termed "Slob Blogging." Sharing the ins and outs of my deepest, darkest, most embarrassing secret with the world has been a long and often painful process, but I'm thankful. Focusing on my home and analyzing my whys and why-nots has worked. I understand now.

I know what it takes to manage my home without losing my mind.

If you're still reading and you haven't made up your mind yet about whether this book is for you, I'll spell it out:

If you want to learn from the best, I'm not the best. If you want to clean your house from top to bottom and never have to clean it again, I'm not your woman. If you're looking for tips that will help you tweak your already almost-perfect organizing strategies, move right along.

But if you want to finally understand what it takes to bring (and keep) your own home out of Disaster Status, this is the book for you. If you've cried real tears of pain and isolation because you *just don't get it*, you've found your people.

I get it.

Here's the dirty little secret about most organizing advice: It's written by organized people. Their brains don't work like mine.

I know what it takes to change. I know because I've done it. Every strategy I'm going to share with you has been tested and proven in my own Slob Lab. No hypotheses, just real life. These ways work, even when life happens. There's no perfection here, no fairy tales. Just clear explanation of what you need to do to get your real-life home under control.

Oh. And I'm funny.

Part I

Reality Check

My First Step: Giving Up on the Fantasy

Fantasy: I struggle to keep my home under control. I'm chronically disorganized or organizationally challenged.
Reality: I'm a slob.

In almost every fairy tale, someone cleans. Most of the princesses do housework during the story, but that's before they are (or *know* they are) princesses. They make cleaning look fun. They sing and dance, and the dust never sends them into sneezing fits or makes their eyes swell shut. But once the prince arrives, cleaning's over. Life is all about fancy dinners and sitting on thrones and smiling at peasants out of carriage windows and such.

Basically, they clean before they arrive at their destinies. Once they're there, cleaning is irrelevant. Nobody talks about cleaning or worries about cleaning or even notices cleaning is happening. But everything stays clean.

Even though I would have told you I knew life wasn't a fairy tale, when it came to cleaning, I embraced this delusion. I was confident that one day cleaning would be easy. My house would stay clean without me even realizing I was cleaning it.

So what awakened me from this delusionary dream?

My messy house.

My grown-up, married-woman, I'm-the-mama house.

I'd been messy since birth. I had a messy room as a child, a messy desk in elementary school, a messy locker in high school, and a messy dorm room in college.

I had apartments with roommates and by myself. All of them were messy.

In case you aren't convinced, I'm talking about more than folded laundry not being put away in a timely manner. Let me paint the (messy) picture.

My living spaces were shockingly messy. People who assured me they wouldn't be shocked were so shocked they couldn't hide it. *And all my college friends were actors.*

I'm talking about the kind of messy where you forget the color of the carpet. The kind of messy where you finally give up and eat off paper plates and drink from disposable cups.

And still the sink is full of dirty dishes 99.9 percent of the time.

This kind of messy makes you pretend you enjoy talking outside in freezing weather when someone stops by unexpectedly.

This kind of messy lets "I tripped over a pile" be an acceptable explanation for a broken toe.

But as I waded through the mess, I felt confident the day would come when I would no longer be messy. I didn't worry that that day hadn't yet arrived. It would happen when it mattered. Once I achieved my life goal of being a stay-at-home mom, everything would be easy. My house would be clean.

Reality hit once I was at that point, living in my grown-up house with nothing to do but be a wife and a mom, and my house wasn't clean.

I was baffled.

I tried. I cleaned like a madwoman until I dropped in exhaustion, but as soon as I congratulated myself on my permanently changed ways, I looked up to see the mess was back.

I could get my home under control for a week, sometimes two, occasionally three weeks at a time. Life would happen, and the house went back to being a disaster.

4

I created the blog *A Slob Comes Clean* eight years after I arrived at the place in life where cleaning was supposed to be easy. I started on what I now call my *deslobification journey* in that moment of desperation in 2009. I did not want to use the s-word. I'd often told myself and others that no matter how bad it was, I was *not* a slob.

But that was the word that came to me. The word that worked.

A Slob Comes Clean is a catchy title and rather self-explanatory. I was ready to be honest with myself, and I was ready to get my house under control.

Still, it's an insult. The dictionary defini-tion is clear. You don't call someone a slob if you want to be her friend.

And that's why it worked. Once I called myself a slob, I couldn't sugarcoat my "issues" anymore. I stopped making excuses.

There's another reason I'm glad I used that awful word. It helped me find my people. As women started reading my blog, they weren't horrified. Instead, they thanked me. These

> I was ready to be honest with myself, and I was ready to get my house under control.

women were relieved to find someone who thought and struggled the way they did, and they were glad to know they weren't alone.

As I learned more about these women who shared my struggles, I saw they were amazing, creative, intelligent people. They were artists and poets and teachers and musicians.

I *liked* them.

Over time, by connecting with women who told me the thoughts I expressed were their thoughts, too, I identified a relationship between the slob part of my brain (the part I despised) and the creative part of my brain (the part I loved). Knowing the direct relationship between these two sides helped me accept that being a slob is part of who I am. It's how my brain works. This realization did not mean I should give up, but it did give me permission to stop feeling like a failure when traditional organizing advice (written by people whose brains are very different from mine) didn't work for me. I just needed to find ways that worked for me, with my unique brain and in my unique home.

2

The Worst Thing About the Best Way

Fantasy: If something is worth doing, it's worth doing right.

Reality: While I'm busy searching for the best way to do something, I'm not getting anything done. Meanwhile, the problem gets worse and is much harder to solve when I finally get around to solving it.

Not all idealists are slobs, but most slobs are idealists.

I'm one. An idealist. (And, of course, a slob.)

I love a good idea. Give me a problem to solve, and I'll start brainstorming solutions. Efficiency and practicality and all that? *They speak to the depths of my soul.*

Before I actually had a home of my own, I couldn't imagine a reason to *not* do things (*all* things, every last little thing) the very best way.

When I was sixteen, I worked at a summer camp. This camp was my favorite place on earth. I loved it so much I even smiled as I cleaned toilets.

I knew how to clean those bathrooms thoroughly, and I cleaned them every single day of the weeks I was assigned bathroom duty. I followed step-by-step lists that told me exactly what to do. I also had lists for every other job I was assigned. Mopping the kitchen? Dusting the chapel? No swish or scrape was left off these lists.

My idealist self was happy. I was learning the very best way to clean, and I was going to *rock* being a homemaker one day. I would do everything right. *All* the time! I mean, I was cleaning those showers perfectly at the camp in the two hours each day when I had nothing else to do but clean bathrooms, so of course I'd do it all perfectly when I had one little ol' bathroom of my own (maybe two) to clean.

At the same camp, I worked in the kitchen, washing dishes and serving food. We learned in one of our health trainings that it's actually more hygienic to let dishes air-dry than to dry them with a dish towel. At least that's the part I remember.

I'm pretty sure the point was to be vigilant about using superclean, totally dry cloths to dry dishes. Y'know, since it would be impractical to let everything air-dry.

I didn't pay attention to the part about it being impractical. Impracticality? That's for wimps! Wusses! Why would I ever do anything other than what was best?

Years later, now that I'm living smack-dab in the middle of reality, I've realized my desire for the very best way contributes to my slob problem.

Huh? Well, this:

What's that? Oh, just a bunch of baking sheets, slow-cooker parts, soup pots, movie theater refillable cups (and more) . . . air-drying.

Air-drying for ~~days weeks~~ months at a time.

Here's what happens: I let them air-dry because air-drying is the very best way. I learned that from the *professionals*.

Plus, air-drying means I don't have to find a dish towel, I don't have to dry each one individually, and I don't have to put them away right now. I *can't* put them away right now. They're *air-drying*. Duh.

The very best way is also the easiest way? What could possibly be better than that?

Except that if air-drying is going to be the very best way, it has to include putting the dishes away. But air-drying takes time. It doesn't happen immediately. And no one (especially no one who considers herself superefficient) can be expected to watch dishes dry.

But by the time the dishes are dry, they've blended into the landscape of my kitchen counters. They've been there long enough they don't register to my brain as being out of place.

The next time I need a baking sheet, I grab it. I use it, wash it, and put it back in the pile to air-dry, because air-drying is the very best way.

It seems normal and not at all lazy until one day I feel inexplicable despair. I stand in my kitchen, wondering why I feel so bad, and suddenly realize I'm irritated by its overall messy appearance.

I shake my head to clear my Slob Vision and realize there's a huge pile of stuff behind my sink.

An eyesore I didn't see with my eyes but felt with my heart.

Sometimes, Worrying About the Very Best Way Keeps Me from Doing Anything

I stress and fret over the very best way to clean my toilet, worrying I'll ruin my health or the environment or my children's lives. While I'm worrying, the toilet gets ickier. And harder to clean. So, eventually, when I have to clean that toilet because it's just so gross (and Grandma's on her way over),

I have no choice but to use scarier stuff than the cleaning products I was scared to use in the first place.

It's a cycle. A bad one.

While I tell myself I'm going to look up the best way to recycle in my area, my recycling container overflows and turns into a recycling "area." The plastic bottles and newspapers eventually mix with other junk that's not recyclable.

Now it's a *project*. A frustrating, overwhelming project I put off even longer, so it grows.

And becomes more overwhelming.

Things should be done a certain way. Why do something at all if there's a better way it could be done? But even if I knew a better way, would I have the supplies or the time to do it that way?

Three words in that last paragraph are ones I now recognize as signal words: *would*, *could*, and *should*. Signals that it's never going to happen. When those words are in my inner monologue, I have to ask myself, "But what *will* I do?"

> All the wouldas, couldas, and shouldas in the world don't get my bathroom clean. Know what gets it clean? Cleaning it.

All the wouldas, couldas, and shouldas in the world don't get my bathroom clean. Know what gets it clean? Cleaning it. (Seriously, the profundity in this book is amazing.) When I called myself a slob, I had no choice but to face reality. My ensuing passion for reality has been a big factor in my own deslobification process. I accepted that whatever I had been doing in my home wasn't working. Ideas weren't making a difference. The only thing that made a difference was actually doing something. Cleaning with whatever I had on hand, whether it was the perfect thing or not.

Over time, and with much angst, I can now more easily differentiate Really Great Ideas from Things That Might Actually Happen in My House. With success and progress, I'm willing to act on realistic ideas and not bother with the ones that will never happen.

Need an Example of Things That Will Never Happen?

I saw a fascinating tip from my friend Lauren, who writes about living frugally at iamthatlady.com. She shared that people sell empty toilet paper rolls on eBay.

I'm not kidding. I checked, and it's for real. The auctions I found finished with a buyer paying between five and fifteen dollars for fifty to one hundred empty, "clean" toilet paper rolls.

For someone who uses toilet paper, like, every single day of her life (and hopes everyone else does too), that would be free money! I could save those things, box 'em up, and ship 'em off to the highest bidder! Yee-haw—I should totally do this!

(Signal words alert: *would*, *could*, and *should*—all in the same paragraph.)

In the interest of putting energy and time into only Things That Will Actually Happen, let's play this one out in my slob reality:

I place a handy-dandy box in the bathroom cabinet. "I'll put this in here. That way, whenever we finish a roll of toilet paper, we can drop it in this box!"

I smile to myself, thinking of all the money some sucker's going to pay for my trash.

Three weeks later, I open the cabinet for a completely-unrelated-to-selling-used-toilet-paper-rolls reason.

I think to myself (in a strident tone), *Who put that box in here?* I reach to remove the box and then remember my plan for ultimate high-profit recycling. Oh, yeah. I forgot.

I call the rest of the family into the bathroom. "Okay, everyone, every time you finish a roll of toilet paper, put the empty roll in this box. We are going to sell them!"

Blank stares.

Hubby, wide-eyed, backs me up, "You heard Mom. Don't throw empty toilet paper rolls away." Once the kids are gone, he asks for an explanation. I give one, and he leaves the bathroom, shaking his head.

A month later, I find the box with two empty rolls in it, and I give up.

While there are a ba-jillion good habits we can't seem to create, we're amazing at putting empty toilet paper rolls straight into the trash can without ever thinking about Mom's great idea.

Or maybe it plays out like this:

We get excited about paying for next summer's vacation with money earned from selling used toilet paper rolls to strangers on the Internet. The whole family gets in on the action, and we fill up those boxes until they overflow.

And tumble out of the cabinet when someone opens the door.

We collect more. And more. And even more. The time has finally arrived to sell them.

But I need a camera and a box that will fit all of them without smushing them (since we've overfilled the original box).

And I can't remember my eBay password.

I can solve all those problems, but I'll have to wait until a better time. A time when I have the mental energy to deal with all of that. A time when I simply . . . have more time.

Meanwhile, we gather more and more empty rolls, and I get more overwhelmed, and it becomes less realistic that I'll ever get around to actually doing this.

And we can't use that cabinet because it's overflowing with empty toilet paper rolls.

These scenarios may seem extreme, but they're exactly how it could go down in my house. I know.

Because I know, I choose reality.

Reality is accepting that while some people do things like this and earn decent chump change, selling my trash would be more trouble than it's worth to me. And it would make my house even harder to maintain.

I can't, as a slob, do anything that will make my home harder to maintain.

Instead, I'll view the information like this: "Wow, that is so cool! People *really* sell used toilet paper rolls on eBay? Next time the school/church asks for them, I'll buy some! Yay for having *no* reason to keep boxes full of used toilet paper rolls. Ever!"

Failing at the Very Best Way Makes Me Lose Faith in My Ability to Do It at All

While selling used toilet paper rolls and air-drying dishes for months at a time are obviously unrealistic ideas, I've had to change my idealistic mind-set in more subtle, yet significant, ways.

The biggest housekeeping dream I've had to give up was my unwavering belief that I just needed to find the right method for cleaning my house.

Oh, the elusive method. The answer to all my problems. If I could find the perfect method, my house would be clean all the time.

I have some bad news.

You can read this entire book five times in a row and your house won't be any cleaner than it was before you opened it.

Methods don't clean your house. *You* have to clean your house.

While I'm reading about systems for doing laundry or researching the best way to keep my kitchen under control or asking my neighbor how often she mops her floors, my house is getting messier.

And more overwhelming.

Even worse, when I find a way that seems to work, it eventually stops working.

> Methods don't clean your house. *You* have to clean your house.

Or I stop working. But my focus on the method as the thing that is cleaning my house lets me blame the method—and throw away the method.

Every time I throw away another method, I remember all the other methods that have failed. And my hope for ever finding a method that will work deflates a little more.

I fall deeper into the pit of self-loathing and cynicism and believe I'll never find a way.

But it's not about finding a way. It's about cleaning my house.

3

Bad News: Cleaning Your House Isn't a Project

Fantasy: Someday, when I have a solid month to devote to my house, I'll get it totally cleaned and decluttered. I don't see the point in starting until I know I can finish.

Reality: Housekeeping doesn't end. Ever.

I love a good project.

I love the planning phase, the preparation phase, the creation phase, and the finishing phase.

I taught theatre arts pre-kids. My office at school? A total mess. But my productions on stage were close to perfect. Actors received detailed schedules at the first meeting. Props were traced with marker on butcher paper so I could see at a glance that everything was in place. No guesswork. No loosey-gooseyness tolerated. Most plays involved me kicking out at least one actor who didn't understand I was serious when I said rehearsals were mandatory.

People knew exactly where to be and exactly what to do. If they didn't, we went over the scene six or sixty times—whatever we needed to do to make it perfect.

Projects consume me. I let everything else in my life go on hold, and when I'm done, I stand back and expect (and enjoy) the applause.

This might be why some people who originally knew me as Director Dana have a hard time wrapping their heads around Slob Dana. I mean, someone so obsessed with details like era-appropriate hairstyles doesn't notice the toothpaste she grabbed was sitting in a pile of six empty tubes? How does that make sense?

Here's the thing: as a project lover, I like to finish stuff. I like to work hard and then step away, living the rest of my life with the memory of how awesome I was in that moment. Of the amazing results of my hard work.

I like to finish and move on.

Not much sticks in my craw like redoing something I did right the first time.

But housework/home management/whatever you want to call it *isn't a project.*

It has no end.

Sparkly bathtub? Go you. For, like, an hour until someone takes a bath.

Dishes done? *And* put away? Yippee! We can eat lunch! (And make more dirty dishes!)

These things are irritating to anyone who has ever tried to keep a home running smoothly. But most people manage while they grumble.

I couldn't. My Project Brain is a big part of why I struggle to keep my house under control.

> My house is not a project. Viewing my home as a project does more harm than good.

I viewed my house as a project. My house is not a project. Viewing my home as a project does more harm than good.

I thought I needed to clean my house from top to bottom, backward and forward and inside out. Once I did that, if I could *ever* do that, *then* I could maintain. *Then* I could keep my home under control.

So that's what I did. The cleaning part, not the maintaining.

I knew how to clean my house. I could clean like a maniac. If I had a goal, like a party, I mapped out a plan and followed it until I opened the door to my guests.

I brought them inside (pretending my house always looked this way) and reveled in the beauty of my goal home.

After all that work, all that sweat and stress and angst, I'd swear I was going to keep my home this way. *This* time.

Three days later, I looked around and gasped. My home was worse than it was before I started cleaning for the party. Clutter had reappeared, dishes were piled in the sink, and the floor was scattered with dirty socks.

All that work, and I had been betrayed. My project energy was gone, and my heart was broken once again by my cruelly messy house. With each failure, my cynicism increased. I accepted the hopelessness of my situation a little more.

The problem? Those three days between Party Ready and Disaster Status. They were a black hole in my Slob Brain. I honestly didn't understand what had happened during those three days.

Now I know. I didn't do the boring stuff. Without realizing what I was doing (or not doing), I was waiting for my house to turn into another project I could tackle.

I was waiting for the dishes to pile high enough to justify a project called Stop All the Things I Like to Do and Wash Dishes.

I have Slob Vision. I don't see a few dishes. I don't see incremental mess. I see beautifully clean and overwhelmingly messy, but the in-between doesn't register in my brain. Even if the mess caught my eye at a random time, the scene didn't feel urgent. The entire house was so much better than usual. Shouldn't my reward for "so much better" be *not* doing the dishes?

Part of the joy of a project is not thinking about the project anymore once I'm done. If my entire focus for three weeks before the party was cleaning and purging and *not* letting dishes pile up on the counter, the three days after the party should include not cleaning, not purging, and not worrying about dishes.

But the longer I go between Project Cleanings, the harder and more overwhelming Project Cleanings are, and the longer I put them off.

You know what made the difference? Doing the dishes.

Here's what I had to accept: Cleaning my house is not a project. It's a series of boring, mundane, repetitive tasks. The people whose homes are clean all the time do these boring, mundane, repetitive tasks.

That's a rather depressing reality for someone who is always convinced she has a better way to do everything and who thrives when she's working toward a big finish.

> Here's what I had to accept: Cleaning my house is not a project. It's a series of boring, mundane, repetitive tasks. The people whose homes are clean all the time do these boring, mundane, repetitive tasks.

I'm not an idiot. But my house compared to what I saw of other people's houses made me feel like an idiot. As someone not used to feeling like an idiot, my inability to do what I'd assumed I'd be able to do once I "put my mind to it" was mind-boggling. And depressing. And humiliating.

I finally had to understand that there isn't a better way. The only way to keep the dishes from piling up is to wash them. Really.

But I do have *some* good news.

If you're anything like I was when I started this deslobification process in my own home, you have no idea what it means to do the dishes.

I thought doing the dishes was a project. The only experience I had doing dishes was setting aside a few hours to clean my kitchen. Usually, this full-day project was the starting point of renewed determination to clean up my messy house. I loaded and reloaded my dishwasher, handwashed every pot and pan we owned, and then couldn't fit it all into the cabinets once everything was clean. (More fodder for a messiness-induced mental breakdown.)

I didn't know about Dirty Dishes Math: Washing every dish in the house takes hours. But the next day, when there are only ten plates and twelve glasses and three coffee cups and a pasta pot and a skillet, a strange thing happens—everything fits in one load.

One load of dishes takes less than five minutes to empty and five minutes to reload.

Y'all, that's ten minutes.

But two days' worth of dishes doesn't fit in one load, so they take the ten minutes plus handwashing and finagling and counter-shifting, which takes way more than twenty minutes. Three days' worth? We're back to hours and hours.

So the goal becomes doing the dishes every day and preventing the project.

But lest you feel like slamming this book shut in a huff and pouting because I've burst your project-loving bubble, here's a little hope for you. A crazy thing happens when you realize the most basic home management stuff isn't a project. When the dishes are done every day (and other stuff, but mostly dishes), and dishes and other stuff are taking *way* less time than they did when they grew to Project Status, time opens up for other projects. Real projects. Ones I *like*. Like painting bathrooms, writing books, and letting my kids plant a garden in the backyard.

Really. It's like magic.

Worried I've oversimplified by saying, "Do the dishes"? Don't worry. I'm about to wear you out on that subject.

Part 2

Daily Stuff:
The Down-and-Dirty
Truth About a Clean House

4

Where to Start

Fantasy: There's just . . . so . . . much . . . to do. I'm
overwhelmed, so I'll make a list. A big, long, detailed list.

Reality: I lost the list.

I don't even know where to start."
I hear this statement all the time, and I understand.

Home management isn't a project, but for someone like me, when the
entire house is one big out-of-control mess, it looks and feels (and, honestly,
sometimes *smells*) like a project.

When I started this deslobification process, I was desperate. Defeated.
My only hope was that blogging about it would help me focus.

I didn't know where to start, but I knew what I'd been doing didn't
work. I continually found myself back in the same mess, never gaining any
traction or making real progress.

I decided to start small. As small and underwhelming as possible. I was
desperate *not* to fail this time.

I decided to do the dishes.

Here was my rationale: Every time I got a burst of cleaning energy, I
had to start in the kitchen. A house isn't clean if the kitchen isn't clean. But
my kitchen was a whole-day project. By the time I was done, my elusive

23

cleaning energy had vanished, and I never moved on to the rest of the house.

If I did make it past the kitchen, the kitchen (quite rudely) got messy again while I worked elsewhere.

It was a never-ending cycle.

I had to get this figured out.

I'd seen homes with kitchens that were always clean. I have relatives and friends whose dishes are always done, no matter how unexpected my visit. I just didn't have a clue how they did it.

Since I didn't know what to do, I did the dishes. I knew dishes were the most time-consuming task when I cleaned the kitchen, so if I could figure out how to keep them done, it would help.

Starting small, focusing only on dishes and washing them every day, brought about real progress. Progress I'd never experienced before.

I didn't worry about the whole house. I didn't even worry about "the kitchen." I just focused on the dishes.

And I just *washed* them. I didn't analyze or observe how other people kept their dishes under control before I got started.

I just did the dishes.

The second day, I did them again.

The third day? Again.

My fear of failure was so great that I kept my expectations as low as I possibly could. My goal was simply to do the dishes. Not achieve something each day. Not really even have anything to show for my day. I just needed to do this very small thing.

Something crazy happened. By doing the dishes, I started understanding *how* to do the dishes.

Not that I didn't know how to do them before. I knew how to squirt soap and wash a skillet, but I didn't know how to do dishes as a habit.

When I was single and living in Thailand, I was invited to have dinner in the apartment of an older couple. I watched the woman cook. She moved easily about her kitchen. She was completely comfortable. She confidently reached for the seasoning, grabbed it without reading the label, and sprinkled it into the pan without stressing over how much she needed. As someone who was currently in love and dreaming of marriage, but who was living alone and awkwardly learning to cook, I admired her so much and hoped I would one day be at ease in my own kitchen.

At the point I started the blog, I was at ease with cooking, but doing the dishes every day, not as a marathon cleaning session, was awkward to me.

My hand didn't know exactly where to go to grab the dish soap. Who knew where I'd left it at the end of the last exhausting dishwashing session? Then, there's the whole matter of stopping my day to do a few dishes. Pausing my busy Mom Life for a barely-even-a-pile in the sink.

I gave myself the same pep talk I'd given my drama students and my own kids over the years: Most things that look easy are skills. Skills can be learned.

As someone born with a flair for the dramatic, I got involved in theatre because it came naturally to me. I remember, though, in college, being surprised at how much there was to learn about acting. I saw something that served Future Teacher Me well. I saw people to whom acting didn't come naturally . . . learn. I saw them work hard. I watched them turn into excellent actors because they learned the skills they needed to be excellent actors.

Some kids get on a soccer field at the age of four and amaze everyone with their natural talent. The other kids stand and watch and occasionally pluck a dandelion. But if you watch those same kids at age twelve, you'll never know that the kid running down the field, weaving in and out with finesse, and driving to the goal was once a dandelion picker. She stuck with it, her confidence grew, and she learned the skills she needed to be successful.

Some people pick up a guitar or sit down at a piano and start playing. Those people are rare. Most musicians spend hours and hours every week for years to learn the skills that make people think they're naturals.

Once you have a well-practiced skill, it looks easy, but making something look easy takes a lot of hard work.

As I did the dishes every day—every single day, whether the number of dishes seemed worth doing or not—it stopped feeling so awkward. For one thing, once I grasped Dirty Dishes Math and knew I'd be done in minutes rather than hours, I didn't have to waste time slumping my shoulders and groaning ~~inwardly~~ audibly. I didn't have to give myself a pep talk (as often) to get started. I didn't waste time standing in the middle of the kitchen, staring at piles of dishes, wondering how my home got this bad again, and coming up with a new plan because the old one obviously didn't work.

I just did the dishes.

Because I have a dishwasher, this meant unloading it, putting away yesterday's load, and reloading it with dirty dishes.

Over weeks of focusing on not failing at this one simple, low-expectation task, I figured out the rhythm and timing that works for our family. After the first week, doing the dishes wasn't easy, but it wasn't completely overwhelming. I decided to add another thing.

So I looked around my kitchen and thought about what drove me craziest. What seemed to *always* be a problem?

Tripping.

Stuff was always on the floor. Newspapers from last week. Napkins dropped by the kids. A piece of broccoli the dog didn't want.

I decided I would sweep the floor every day. The first day, sweeping the floor was a project, just like it had always been. "Sweeping" was picking up newspapers, putting away the last few groceries that were sitting in grocery bags on the floor, throwing away the wrapper from the package of paper towels we opened yesterday. It was bending over and picking up and throwing out and putting away. Sweeping was a project.

Every corner, every under-the-counter space, every under-the-chair area had to be cleared of toys and random clutter so I could sweep.

The kitchen looked so good after all that work.

With an empty sink, a clear counter, and a free-of-clutter floor, my kitchen looked like a normal person's kitchen. Like one I wouldn't be embarrassed to show a visitor.

But like the dishes, the good stuff happened on the second day. The second day, sweeping wasn't a project. It was an amazingly quick chore. Pick up a random napkin and sweep the floor.

The next day was the same, and the next day again. When I swept every day, sweeping the floor wasn't the least bit overwhelming.

At the time when all this was new to me and I had no idea if I was doing it right, my blog was a secret. A few weeks after I started, I was with a friend who knew about my dream of blogging. She asked if I'd started yet.

I didn't want to lie, but I was okay with being vague. I said, "Mmm-hmm."

She asked what it was about. Again with the vagueness, I told her it was a practice blog I was using to get my house under control. Her son and my son played together. She'd seen my house. She knew this was a problem for me.

She asked what I was doing, and I mumbled something about starting small and how I was sweeping my kitchen every single day, no matter what.

She said, "Oh. I don't sweep my kitchen every day." Kind of like she felt bad about that. Like maybe she should start. I'd seen her house on random days. She was fine doing whatever she'd been doing. She definitely didn't need to model anything related to housekeeping after me.

I explained this was what *I* had to do. I didn't know if it was the right thing, but I knew it was helping me a lot.

A few weeks later, on a Monday morning, as I started the nonnegotiable task of sweeping my kitchen, I realized why I need to sweep my kitchen every day even though not everyone does.

The task had very little to do with sweeping my kitchen. It was about the pile of newspapers on the floor by the breakfast table. I didn't even see them until I grabbed my broom.

Having a nonnegotiable task cleared my Slob Vision. I saw the clutter because I couldn't sweep the kitchen without seeing it.

Sweeping the kitchen when the floor is so cluttered I can't walk without tripping is a project. Sweeping the kitchen every day is a two-minute (four, tops) task. Even when the task involves picking up one or two previously invisible items off the floor.

Weeks into my deslobification process, I was learning that habits were the way to go. Habits were making a much bigger impact than I ever thought possible.

So I kept going. I added a new habit once the last one started to feel natural. Not easy, but natural.

Generally, new habits felt natural(ish) in a week.

If you want a day-by-day, step-by-step guide, "28 Days to Hope for Your Home" is an appendix at the end of this book. It's an instructional guide to developing four habits that will have a major impact on your home. More major than you could ever imagine.

Or you can just pick a habit. Here's how I chose: I looked around my house and decided what made me the most anxious. Not anxious like who-put-that-cup-there-I-never-leave-cups-there anxious, but anxious like "How do other people not have this happen, but for me it's a constant frustration?"

Maybe your frustration is the shoe pile at the back door. Maybe the books that never get put back on the bookshelf irritate you.

Choose whatever drives you crazy, whatever seems unsolvable.

If your dishes are always clean, don't switch to my method of doing them. Choose something that's a problem in your own home. My friend had no reason to start sweeping her kitchen every day if she naturally noticed when it was dirty and then swept it.

> That's *all* that matters: finding what works in your home for your unique family.

Solve your chosen problem today. Then, and this is the key, solve it again tomorrow, before it's a problem again.

Solve it when "solving" only involves a little straightening or a little shifting or one quick wipe with a cloth. Solve the same problem every day for seven days. After seven days, you'll have tried multiple solutions, and one of them will work. That's *all* that matters: finding what works in your home for your unique family.

Slight Preaching Break for Those Who Don't Have Dishwashers

I feel the time has come to address those who have rolled their eyes and heavy-sighed in disgust at my encouragement to do the dishes. Don't worry—I can't actually see you. I know your reaction, though, because I have years of Slob Blogging market research under my belt.

When I mention running the dishwasher, or emptying it, or anything at all to do with having one, people without dishwashers tend to complain. They say, "[Sigh] I wish I *had* a dishwasher." Or "Must be nice to have a dishwasher." Or "This might help if I actually *had* a dishwasher!"

I get it. I love my dishwasher a little too passionately. I have also lived without one for years at a time and was confident *not* having a dishwasher was the cause of all my housekeeping problems.

Let me say something truly profound: if you don't have a dishwasher, you live in a house without a dishwasher.

Hate me more? I'm not belittling your problems, and I would personally put a good dishwasher above many other amenities when searching for a home, but a dishwasher did not get my kitchen under control. I did.

What solved my dishwashing problems? Washing the dishes.

For years, my kitchen was a constant mess while I had a perfectly good dishwasher. I know multiple people (my mother-in-law, my sister-in-law, a close friend whose home I visit regularly) who do not use dishwashers. Their kitchens are clean. In fact, when the friend finally got a dishwasher after years of handwashing, she complained that her kitchen was messier than it had ever been before because her routine was messed up. The dishwasher made the actual action of taking dishes from dirty to clean easier but did nothing to keep her kitchen under control.

Having a dishwasher or not having a dishwasher isn't the issue. Having a routine or not having a routine is the issue. People with consistently clean kitchens have routines, whether or not they have dishwashers. Dirty Dishes Math still applies to handwashed dishes. Don't wash dishes today, and tomorrow's task will require six times more effort.

If bedtime is a deadline for washing dishes, putting handwashed dishes away the next morning is as important as emptying a dishwasher. Just like an empty dishwasher makes putting newly dirtied dishes straight into it seem logical, an empty sink and an empty dish-drying rack make washing a single dish seem logical as well.

And more than anything, lamenting the lack of a dishwasher in a house that doesn't have a dishwasher does absolutely nothing to improve that house. Wishing, planning, and crying have never improved a home. I know. I was the queen of wishing and planning and crying.

The only way to have a clean kitchen is to clean it. The only way to keep a kitchen in a state where it's easy to clean is to do the dishes every single day, whether you have a dishwasher or not.

Wow. That little preaching break was a little obnoxious. Sorry. I promise to be nicer in the next chapter.

. . . .

Proof It's Not Just Me
(Stories from readers at ASlobComesClean.com)

Throughout the book, at the end of most chapters, I'll share stories from blog readers and podcast listeners at ASlobComesClean.com. Partly, I'm proving that I'm not the only one who has these struggles! But mostly, I love sharing evidence that these strategies actually do work in real life for real people.

> "Doing the dishes every single day makes a world of a difference, even if you have to weave your way through other stuff to get to the sink. And you'll never be able to comprehend how much of a difference until you just do it."
>
> —Brandi D.

> "I don't have a dishwasher. However, I don't like waking up in the morning to all of the dishes that were dirtied after supper while people were snacking. So even though it's one of my least favorite things to do after 8:00 p.m., I wash the dishes before going to bed. Putting away a dish drainer of clean dishes is a much more pleasant way to start your day than coming face to face with a pile of dirty ones when the day is just starting!"
>
> —Kelly G.

Where to Start

"Just doing the dishes makes a difference and can inspire you to do more, but if it doesn't . . . at least the dishes are done."

—Lucy L.

5

....

The Truth About Habits

Fantasy: I need habits. If I can force myself to have a perfectly clean house every day for a month, I'll have habits. Once I've got habits, I won't even notice I'm vacuuming. Just like I didn't notice I was putting another spoonful of sugar in my coffee.

Reality: I'll never clean my house without knowing I'm cleaning my house. If I wait for that, I'll wait forever. While I wait, my house will get dirtier.

I can pick up a bad habit in three days flat and struggle for years to break it. A good habit, however, causes emotional angst and physical pain to create, but I can break it in less than twenty-four hours.

So maybe it's important to look at good and bad habits differently.

I once thought of habits as things I do without thinking. Like stealing candy out of my kid's Halloween bucket on November 1. A minute ago, I was at my computer, and now I'm standing in a different room stuffing my face with Skittles. I don't even know how I got here.

Bad habits. I have lots of those. I assumed when people talked about cleaning habits they would work the same way, but they don't. They *so* don't.

I have never once found myself dusting and thought, "How in the world did I get here? I don't even remember grabbing the duster!" Each and every cleaning task I do requires full cognitive awareness that I'm doing it. As a slob, I find this discouraging, but understanding this reality has helped me make progress in my home.

In the beginning of my own deslobification process, I called the things I was adding to my daily list *nonnegotiable tasks*. This was what they were in the beginning. I was figuring out which things had to be done daily and not allowing myself to negotiate my way out of those tasks.

I am a master inside-my-own-brain negotiator. I can/could/do come up with a million reasons why now isn't a good time, why it's logical to wait until the mess is bigger.

At some point, I started calling these nonnegotiables *daily tasks*. I'd whittled them down to the most essential and realized I didn't need to keep adding more. My house was looking *so* much better just from small things I was doing every day. I understood which ones made the biggest impact. I was done negotiating.

When I chose the four most basic tasks that make the biggest impact in "28 Days to Hope for Your Home," I called them *habits*. They felt natural because I did them every single day. They had a place in my day's routine.

Now, I think of these things as *pre-made decisions*. This perspective works for me.

I don't get to decide if certain things need to be done. I know for a fact they do. Just like I don't get to decide the sky is blue.

I got into this mess because I was so good at justifying *not* doing the dishes. I was too busy, there weren't enough dirty dishes to "waste" water, another time would be a better time—whatever came up that sounded the least bit logical so I could get out of doing what I really didn't want to do anyway. My ~~excuses~~ reasons make so much sense in the moment.

So I've removed the decision-making process. I don't get to make a decision about whether I do the dishes every night. I know from experience (the most effective teacher) what I have to do to keep the kitchen under control. But I don't use that knowledge to give myself a pep talk. There's nothing to pep myself up about. There's no decision to make.

Because a decision would go like this: *That's not enough to fill the dishwasher. I should wait until tomorrow.*

But a pre-made decision goes like this: *I don't have a choice. I have to run the dishwasher. Because I have to run it, I have to put those dishes in it. Oh. There were more dishes than I thought. It's almost full.*

If I get that far, but I let myself make a decision, it would go like this: *Well, it's not completely full. I'm pretty sure I could save the planet right here and now if I waited until it was full. Yeah. Waiting is good.*

> I've removed the decision-making process. I don't get to make a decision about whether I do the dishes every night.

But without a decision to make: *It's not completely full, but I have to run it. That's what I do to keep my kitchen under control, so I'm not allowed to decide not to run it. Because I have to run it, I should look around the kitchen to see if I've missed anythi—Oh. How did I not see that pile?*

My entire kitchen benefits from this pre-made decision.

Because I'm running the dishwasher, I should look around the rest of the house for other random dishes. I find random dirty dishes almost every time, and once they're gone, my entire house looks better.

If I let myself make the decision, I'm almost always wrong. The day after I decide not to do the dishes, there are more dishes than can be run in one load, and I'm behind.

Don't worry. I was disappointed, too, when I learned the reason other people's dishes were always done was because they did the dishes every day. It's a total bummer when you realize there really isn't a better way.

. . . .

For Those Still Assuming the Dishwashing Thing Doesn't Apply Because They Don't Have Dishwashers

"We don't have a dishwasher. I resisted and resisted at first,
but I pushed through. Now it feels so much easier, and I don't

feel as resentful. I find myself doing them because I don't want to be doing them the next day when Dishes Math comes into effect and it takes three times as long."

—Stella L.

6

Just Tell Me What to Do

Fantasy: Once I know what to do, then I can do it. I mean, duh.

Reality: To have a clean house, I have to clean it. That's nowhere near as fun as reading about cleaning. I mean, duh.

Some of you flipped to this chapter and are starting here. I totally get it. You're desperate.

So here you go: do the dishes.

Before you check the crease in the spine to see if you could get away with returning this stupid book, I'll explain a little. (But not a lot. That's what the chapters you skipped are for.)

Doing the dishes seems like the dumbest thing to do when you're overwhelmed with a very messy home. Washing dishes feels pointless. Pointless because the people in your house insist on eating multiple times every single day, and every time they do, they use dishes. So even if you wash them right now, they'll be dirty again in a few hours. Or maybe in a few minutes.

The futility is disheartening. Depressing. Maddening. Overwhelming.

But there is a point. Doing the dishes is the first step of this whole

37

change-your-house process. Doing them again tomorrow is where the magic will happen.

If you think this advice is stupid because your dishes are always done, yay for you. For real, I'm not being sarcastic. (Fine, I kind of am.)

But really, if you can skip this first step, be happy you don't have to conquer the biggest thing that most people who feel despair over the state of their home have to conquer. You get to move ahead.

But if your dishes aren't done, especially if last night's dishes are still on the table and you had to wash a skillet so you could scramble eggs this morning, do the dishes now. Even if it takes all the time you have available to devote to this idiotic deslobification process for the day.

> Doing the dishes is the first step of this whole change-your-house process. Doing them again tomorrow is where the magic will happen.

I get that you won't have time to get to anything else and, therefore, won't have gained a bit of traction, and once your family eats dinner tonight, your sink will be full of dishes again.

But do the dishes anyway. Tonight, you'll walk into your kitchen and *just start cooking*. If you don't remember what that's like, it's awesome. You pull a totally clean pot out of the cabinet and place it on the counter without having to shove last night's (or last week's) dirty dishes out of the way. You use a knife you didn't have to handwash on a cutting board that has space around it for your elbows to move.

You'll feel like you're living in a Food Network kitchen.

But the *real* magic happens after dinner.

Do the dishes again.

Something crazy will happen. You'll learn from experience how long it takes to do one meal's worth of dishes. If you're still feeling skeptical, I'm going to guess you have no idea how long doing the dishes actually takes. It's okay. I didn't know either.

And then the *real* real magic (as opposed to just the "real magic") will happen tomorrow morning when you wake up to kitchen counters that are *not* covered in dirty dishes. Which means tomorrow you'll be excited you don't have to wash your dishes, and you'll very likely tackle something else in your house.

The only thing I'm going to tell you (because I get to boss you around since you're reading *my* book) is to do the dishes again tomorrow night. You'll see one little ol' day's worth of dishes isn't overwhelming. Or depressing. Or maddening.

Spend a week doing that (the dishes every night) and then add another task. I recommend sweeping your kitchen every day. Again, the first day will be completely different from the following days.

After another week, start checking your bathrooms for clutter (and removing that clutter when you find it). Once that starts to feel normal after a week, do a five-minute pickup. (A five-minute pickup is exactly what it sounds like, but I'll explain the ins and outs later.)

Lest you think I'm oversimplifying, go to the end of the book (for those of you who have already proven yourselves to not care one little bit about going in order, this is right up your alley). In the appendix, you'll find "28 Days to Hope for Your Home." That guide will lead you through every little step, day by day, excuse by excuse, and frustration by frustration. In four weeks, you'll have hope for your home. I promise it works if you do the work. (I talked about all of this in a previous chapter, in case you missed it.)

7

Pre-made Decisions

Fantasy: I have an analytical mind. I enjoy thinking
through problems and creating solutions that will last

Reality: Sometimes, I turn things into problems that aren't
really problems just because I love thinking so much.

I've already talked about pre-made decisions and how they're another way
to look at habits. But there are more benefits to pre-made decisions, and
in more than just the daily stuff. If you're often overwhelmed, keep reading.
Pre-made decisions are for you.

When my husband and I bought our last car, our must-have feature
was . . . no keys.

We'd spent a few weeks with a keyless rental car, and those weeks were
blissful for one reason: I never lost my keys.

That's a big deal, y'all.

I'm a loser. A key-loser.

Not always, but it goes in spurts that occur in direct relationship to
brain overload. As a Project Person who takes on big tasks with urgent
deadlines, I tend to overload my brain. I don't necessarily know it's happening until I start forgetting things. My brain deletes "trivial" information so
it can handle the big stuff. Unfortunately, my brain considers things like

where I threw my keys to be trivial, deletable information. It also deletes things like football practice ending thirty minutes earlier than usual on Mondays. And that the entire reason I came to the store was that we desperately needed eggs.

It's a scientific reality that our human brains can only handle so much before they start deleting information to make room. At least I think I've heard that somewhere. I know I've experienced it.

So the beauty of a keyless car is not that I save the physical energy of digging around in my purse for my key; rather it's that there's one less thing in my brain. One less thing to remember. One less concern.

My point is not for you to go buy a keyless car. My point is for you to start looking for small ways you can remove worry, stress, and decision-making from your daily life.

We had to buy a car. Between two equal choices, we let our deciding factor be this feature we knew would remove one small stress from our lives.

What can you do to remove small stresses from your life? You can remove decisions about little things that don't deserve daily brain space. When something registers as a recurring annoyance, try making a decision that will prevent it from being an irritation in the future.

> What can you do to remove small stresses from your life? You can remove decisions about little things that don't deserve daily brain space.

I decided not to keep used gift cards. I was tired of not being able to close my wallet because I had so many. I despised (and put off) spending an hour on the phone checking to see which ones still had money on them.

Now when the cashier asks if I want an empty gift card back, I stifle my automatic yes and say no. And sometimes I let it go even if it has seven cents left on it. Or I pass it to the person behind me in line to use for seven cents off his weekly groceries.

One small stress is deleted from my life and my brain, and that frees brain space for things that actually matter.

When I turn daily stuff I should be doing into pre-made decisions, I accomplish the same purpose. By removing certain decisions from my daily life, I'm freeing up brain space.

If I let doing the dishes daily be a decision, that decision takes up space in my brain even though I don't realize that's what is happening. A messy kitchen takes up subconscious brain space because I know I'll have to decide when to clean it. I'll have to decide when to stop doing other things in my busy life to make the time.

A decision that's waiting to be made is stressful, even if I don't realize it's stressing me.

Routines remove the need to make the same decisions over and over again. Knowing I wash dishes every night means I don't worry (even subconsciously) about when I'm going to do the dishes at any other point during the day. Knowing Monday is Laundry Day means I don't think about laundry on Wednesday or Saturday.

What to Do and When to Do It
(No Lists or Schedules Necessary)

Some people love lists. They get a kick out of making one every single morning. I like lists, but I generally wait to make them for big stuff. I like using lists to complete huge projects that need to be broken down into actionable steps.

When I wrote "28 Days to Hope for Your Home," a friend who proofread it asked if I was going to include printable checklists. But checklists didn't feel right. The entire point of building four habits ever so slowly was that they'd feel natural after four weeks, so you wouldn't even *need* a list.

Every day, no matter how busy, has awkward pauses. In these awkward pauses, I think, *I know I should be doing something. But what?*

An ingrained, decision-free list of the utmost basics to keep a home running smoothly helps me use my awkward pauses wisely. When there are five minutes between bringing one kid home from football practice and taking another to dance class, I don't have to make a decision about how to use those five minutes wisely.

I know I need to run my dishwasher every night. It's a fact, not a decision. Since I have to do it, I might as well spend this five-minute awkward pause moving five more minutes toward having that task done. I can move any random dishes on the counter or in the sink into the dishwasher. I can check for stray dishes in the living room. I might as well. I have to do it anyway.

Maybe the sink and counters look great. I can sweep the floor. Or check the bathrooms, or use the time to do my entire five-minute pickup for the day. If there's no decision to make about the first four things on my daily checklist, I don't have to hem and haw and reason and pontificate about where I should start.

And then there are times when life gets so crazy I skip even the most basic, decision-free tasks I know must be done.

Life happens. Mama's focus moves to something other than house-work. (Like, I don't know, writing a book.) Suddenly I wake up and the house is a disaster again.

Again.

But it's different now. I no longer start from scratch. I don't need to come up with a plan. That plan is done, and the decisions have already been made. I know what to do first and what to do next. I know exactly where to start again.

8

Don't Judge a Habit
on the First Day

Fantasy: I've got a great idea! If I could do the dishes/
laundry/bathrooms every day, they'd never get out of control!

Reality: Umm, doing the dishes took me six hours. No one
has six hours a day to spend washing dishes, so obviously
I'm doing something wrong. This idea is stupid.

Don't judge a habit on the first day. Just don't. On day 1, it's not a habit. The first time you do anything feels awkward. Feel awkward, but don't assume you know what you're dealing with until you've done it again and again and again.

Day 1 of doing the dishes looks nothing like day 16.

There are two other habits you'll work on in "28 Days to Hope for Your Home." One is checking your bathrooms for clutter every day. The goal is to train your brain to see things that are out of place and to make cleaning the bathroom significantly easier and less procrastinatable because it will no longer require thirty minutes of decluttering before you even start. Like doing your dishes daily and sweeping the kitchen, this habit gets easier by the second day.

45

The fourth habit is different, though. It's as quick the first time as it is the twenty-eighth, but you still can't judge it on day 1. I call it the *five-minute pickup*.

While I didn't see the point in doing a few dishes, I always knew I was missing out by not having a designated "pickup" time in our day.

I saw multiple friends go through elaborate bedtime rituals with their kids. Baths and kid shows and evening snacks varied, but the one thing they all did (those friends whose homes were never out of control) was an evening pickup time. The living room was cleared of the day's randomness, and kids' rooms were cleaned of that day's mess.

I tried. I really did try.

So many times I told my family we were starting a new routine. We were going to start cleaning up the living room each night before bedtime. The first night took an hour. It was a major cleanup, and no one bothered to remind me about our new routine the next night. Not long after, I would suddenly realize it had been a week (sometimes *three* weeks) since the thought of picking up the living room had even crossed my mind.

When I started my deslobification process, I knew I had to start doing a daily pickup.

Due to my intense dislike of such things, I chose five minutes. It was, quite literally, the shortest amount of time I could justify devoting to this task. I set the timer on my oven for five minutes and started moving through the house, picking things up and putting them away. When the timer went off, I stopped.

And that right there is the thing that makes this habit different from the others.

Doing dishes the first day can take hours. It's brutal. But on the first day, a five-minute pickup takes only five minutes. However, if your house is in Disaster Status, five minutes may not make a huge impact.

Doing the dishes focuses on one thing you can finish. A five-minute pickup focuses on the entire house, and I hope we've established that thinking you're going to get the entire house completely in order on the first day is a recipe for failure.

If the shock factor of the other habits is how easy they are when done every day, the shock factor of the five-minute pickup is that its impact increases exponentially with each day. On the first day, you're dealing with the top layer of trash and random things that are obviously out of place. That's all you have time to get to in five minutes. On the second day, you get through that top layer more quickly, so you go a little deeper. The next day, you go deeper again, and you might even find yourself dealing with things you once thought were daunting tasks. Maybe you move into the kids' rooms or start folding the clean laundry that has been piled on the love seat for months.

> The shock factor of the five-minute pickup is that its impact increases exponentially with each day.

But you only do these things for five minutes. And each day, you believe more and more in the power of those five minutes.

Involving the Family

I haven't talked much yet (don't worry, there's an entire chapter coming) about involving the other people who live in your home. But I need to mention it now because the five-minute pickup is the perfect habit to turn into a family task.

But, again, don't judge this family habit on the first day. The first day won't be pretty. I don't recommend making *your* first day *their* first day. Let them see you setting the timer and working for five minutes. Be the example of how this works, the proof that we're really only talking about five minutes and not the frantic whole-house-clean-up-before-Grandma-arrives that they're used to.

But even if they've seen (and actually noticed) you doing daily five-minute pickups, that first time as a family will be rough and not the least bit fun.

Your otherwise intelligent children may claim to have never known where scissors or glue or toothpaste go. They will suddenly feel exhausted and suffer headaches and leg pain, and they may stare blankly past your shoulder in confusion when you remind them where you've kept the laundry hamper for all the days of their lives.

The first day will be horrible. Working together, you'll get significantly less done than if you had done it by yourself. You'll spend the entire time directing and reminding and ~~threatening~~ motivating.

But the second day will be a tiny bit better, and the third, slightly better. Eventually, after they've realized this wasn't an isolated Mama's-decided-to-clean incident and after they've done it enough times to realize you really will let them stop after five minutes, you'll fall head over heels in love with the Whole Family Five-Minute Pickup.

Because that is when you will experience Pickup Math, which is totally different from Dirty Dishes Math. Once your family gets the concept and can help without your constant supervision, five minutes multiplies. Now, when I set the timer for five minutes, twenty to twenty-five minutes of work happen. Me plus three kids (and my husband, if he's home) working for five minutes makes a twenty-five minute impact on our home.

Y'all, if we've been rocking our daily habits, we can be ready to have guests over in five minutes.

Five minutes is most definitely worth your time.

The When and the What-If

The perfect time to work a five-minute pickup into your day is *whenever you think of it*. I still, after six years of focusing on this stuff, never think to do a pickup at bedtime. Ever.

If I designate a time for this task to happen, and then I miss that time, I kick myself and make a mental note to remember the next day. But I have some seriously tough shins and am forever misplacing my mental notes, so the days go on and I miss my designated Perfect Pickup Time again and again. The best thing I ever did was decide there *wasn't* a perfect pickup time. It just needed to happen at some point. Whenever I'm working through the basic daily tasks that keep my home under control, I do a five-minute pickup. As long as it happens, my home improves.

But what if, even when I give myself permission to do the five-minute pickup whenever it comes to mind, I still miss it? Three days or three weeks go by.

There's no catching up with this task. Five minutes is still five minutes.

Mandatory catch-ups will happen. Your mother will need a place to stay on her way to a gardening convention, or your friends will ask for a volunteer to host a baby shower. But every five-minute pickup is a small deposit in your clean house account.

Don't judge this habit, or any habit, on the first day. Judge it on the day when you don't have a panic attack at the thought of opening your front door and letting people into your home.

> Don't judge this habit, or any habit, on the first day. Judge it on the day when you don't have a panic attack at the thought of opening your front door and letting people into your home.

9

How to Use Timers: Fighting TPAD (Time Passage Awareness Disorder)

> **Fantasy:** I simply don't have the time right now to do (fill in the blank with whatever I don't want to do right now).
> **Reality:** I have no concept of time. I assume I have too much or too little, whichever lets me not do what I don't want to do.

We've established I resist the mundane. Tasks like doing dishes and picking up random clutter wear me out and will never appear at the top of my list of things I want to do. I've put systems in place and removed decisions in an effort to make these things happen anyway, but then there are the bigger things. Things that don't get done every day but still have to happen.

Things like cleaning bathrooms and mopping floors and dusting. All so irritating, but all so necessary. Even though they don't have to be done every day, they are still never-ending. Nothing stays clean. The minute dust is gone, more settles.

Two things can happen. Some people dust nonstop. They mop three times a day. It never ends, so they never stop. *I'm not one of those people.* While they can't stop, I question the point of starting. Why get down on my knees and scrub behind the toilet when the Night Pee-er is going to strike again before I wake up tomorrow?

I know cleaning has to be done. But because it isn't a project, and it has no end, I put off starting.

I suffer from Time Passage Awareness Disorder (a totally made-up-by-me disorder). TPAD causes me either to put off starting something because I'm sure it will take more time to finish than I have available or to underestimate the time something will take and get in trouble because I put it off, assuming I'll have plenty of time.

Every time I underestimate, the frustration I feel makes me over-estimate the next time. It's a vicious cycle.

Either way, I'm estimating. While estimating is a valid technique for things like adding milk to the gravy, I should give up on it after the sixty-seventh time it fails me in my quest to keep my bathrooms clean.

I fight TPAD with timers. They're a great way to remind myself to start or stop doing something. Nothing good comes from leaving chicken sizzling on the stove while I run to the other side of the house to do something "real quick."

Timers can also be a great tool to make myself get started. They limit the time I'll "have to" keep working. A daily five-minute pickup makes a huge difference, and I'm willing to do it when I know I'll be done in five minutes.

> I need to know for a fact how long certain tasks take so I don't let my TPAD do what it does so well: justify procrastination.

But those are not the main ways I use timers. I use them as reality checkers. I need to remove my estimates. I need to know for a fact how long certain tasks take so I don't let my TPAD do what it does so well: justify procrastination.

Imagining something will take more time than I have? A great reason to procrastinate.

Imagining something won't take long at all? A great reason to procrastinate.

I time myself doing all sorts of things. It works.

When my best friend was in college, she took a Home Economics class. For an assignment, she had to estimate the time required to do each step of a cooking project. The first step was to turn on the light and put on your apron.

She answered . . . ten minutes.

Obviously, she has a touch of TPAD, even though it doesn't affect her home the way it does mine. Hers always looks great. But her answer demonstrates this strange effect of being forced to think about the time it takes to do things you don't normally stop to consider in terms of time. I mean, who even thinks about how long it takes to put on an apron and turn on the light? I never wear an apron (and I'd have to factor in more than ten minutes if my life depended on finding one), and the light is already on. Much to my husband's dismay, I never remember to turn it off.

And in my friend's college-aged mind, a short, inconsequential amount of time was ten minutes. So inconsequential that it's the length of time she wrote down, without thinking through the reality of ten minutes.

I guess that was the point of the exercise. Timing is important, even in everyday things like preparing meals and cleaning kitchens. And if timing is important, it's worth considering.

Ten minutes is a really long time when you're doing jumping jacks and a really short time when you need a nap. Basically, it's a long time for something I don't want to do and a short time for something I do want to do.

If I find myself consistently putting something off, I'll time myself doing it. I hate doing this thing, so it feels endless. Sometimes, realizing how un-endless it is helps me decide I don't hate it as much as I thought I did.

My best example is emptying the dishwasher. Oh, how I hate emptying the dishwasher. But as I got my dishwashing routine down, I realized the importance of this irritating step. Emptying the dishwasher is as important as running it. If I empty it first thing in the morning, I can refill it all day as dishes get dirty. I never even put them in the sink. This keeps my kitchen from getting out of control.

But even after I understood the impact, I put off emptying the dishwasher. I hated doing it, and my hatred caused me to imagine I didn't have time.

I estimated the task took fifteen minutes. Some mornings I legitimately do not have fifteen minutes to spare. If I'm making lunches and finding shoes and putting hair in ponytails, a fifteen-minute, life-doesn't-technically-depend-on-it task may have to wait.

And then something my mother once said came back to me. She told me to time myself doing things I hate doing, just to get a realistic idea of how long those things actually take.

So I timed myself emptying the dishwasher. It took four minutes.

Four little ol' minutes.

My excuses were dashed to smithereens. I can fit four minutes into pretty much any point in my day. It's harder to tell myself I don't have the time when I know for a fact that emptying the dishwasher only takes four minutes.

> Knowing the time required to complete a dreaded task gives me a realistic idea of how to fit the task into my life.

I timed other tasks. I timed myself cleaning bathrooms, vacuuming the living room, dusting the entire house. It's kind of like a game. Not a fun one, but a game.

Knowing the time required to complete a dreaded task gives me a realistic idea of how to fit the task into my life. I'm no longer able to conveniently stretch or compact my understanding of time according to whether I want to do something.

But sometimes it goes the other way. I think I need five minutes to clean out my car before I pick up my kids' friends. I put off getting started until five minutes before I have to leave, only to learn the mess needs a half hour to clean up.

Timing myself cleaning out the car is a reality check. I learn how long it takes to clean a certain volume of mess, and this motivates me not to let it get to a thirty-minute mess the next time.

Knowing Versus Assuming

When I assume, bad things happen.

My TPAD causes me to assume I have plenty of time to wash and dry a load of laundry, but that assumption means my kid is stuck wearing a more-than-slightly damp uniform to his basketball game on Saturday morning.

Or I put off wiping fingerprints and toddler slobber from the glass front door because I assume the irritating task will take forever. When I *have* to clean it in the thirty seconds before friends arrive, I realize I could have done it earlier, almost as quickly but without breaking a sweat or feeling frazzled just before I greet my guests.

Assuming I know how long something will take doesn't work. My assumptions turn into delusions. Timers are a delusion-breaking tool.

. . . .

Proof It's Not Just Me

"I thought I could not do something if I didn't have an hour to do it in. . . . Did you know even the biggest load of laundry takes less than 4 minutes (without rushing) to fold and most loads take far less than that? Nothing takes as long as I thought it did, *and* it feels so good to get it done!"

—Sheila N.

"I didn't want to deal with putting away awkward pieces like canning jars and lids, funnels, blender parts, and various other things I really didn't have a home for. I found if I set the timer for a mere 5–10 minutes after the dishwashing was done, I could focus on dealing with the countertop clutter. If this is done regularly, the mountain of put-off tasks whittles down and then disappears. Setting the timer keeps me focused and on track."

—Vicki W.

10

Putting an End to the Never-Ending: Weekly Cleaning Tasks

Fantasy: I love freshly scrubbed bathrooms and newly mopped kitchen floors. This love should translate into making sure they're scrubbed and mopped regularly. Once a week sounds right.

Reality: I may love clean floors, but I don't notice they need to be mopped until my foot sticks to them.

I don't make good cleaning decisions.

When my daughter was four, I helped scoop ice cream for a party at my older kids' school. The party was held in the cafeteria after all the lunch periods were over. As another mother and I arranged syrups and sprinkles, my talkative preschooler asked the janitor what she was doing.

She was mopping.

My daughter proceeded to ask question after question about why someone would mop and what was involved, like it was a fascinating custom from a different country.

Thankfully, the other mother just laughed, but I felt the need to defend myself. I let my indignation show (with a smile): "I mop every single Thursday!"

Now the other mother looked confused. She remarked she doesn't have a set day for mopping. "I guess I depend on my . . . Cleaning Intuition." I doubt she capitalized those words in her head, but they were immediately capitalized in mine.

Cleaning Intuition is a thing, and I don't have it. As I think about what I want to do over the course of a day, mopping the floor doesn't naturally come to mind. I don't notice when my kitchen needs to be mopped until I find out my mother-in-law is on her way to my house. Or my foot sticks to the floor.

On an ordinary day, "mopping" is just a nagging feeling.

When mopping occurs to me as an "I should really do that" idea, my brain starts wondering how long it has been. Days? Definitely no. Weeks? I wonder how many. Months? Ugh. It may have been a few.

I started my deslobification journey in August 2009, and when the New Year hit with its natural I'm-gonna-change-and-this-time-I-really-mean-it energy, I reflected on the huge improvement I'd made in my home. With only daily nonnegotiables, I was making progress and gaining traction, and I had hope.

> I don't notice when my kitchen needs to be mopped until I find out my mother-in-law is on her way to my house. Or my foot sticks to the floor.

But major cleaning tasks like scrubbing toilets and dusting were still inspiration-dependent. Granted, my inspiration was more frequent because I was blogging about it, and the thought of mopping was significantly less overwhelming because I didn't have to remove several weeks' worth of clutter first.

But inspiration-dependent cleaning has its downfalls. I get busy, and cleaning inspiration eludes me for long periods of time. Long, immeasurable-to-my-Slob-Brain periods of time.

It's TPAD rearing its ugly head again.

I struggle to have any awareness whatsoever of how much time has passed since I last did something. You know that feeling when someone posts a picture on social media and everyone comments how shocked they are that it's been three years since so-and-so was born or city hall caught on fire? It seems like it happened yesterday because the event was a big deal, something out of the ordinary. That's how I viewed big cleaning tasks. Cleaning the bathroom was a momentous occasion, so once I'd done it, I felt like I'd *just* done it. For the next several weeks.

"Didn't I just do that?" was a frequent question in my head—and often out loud.

I needed ~~a better way~~ a way to be consistent with big cleaning tasks that had to be done but were easily put-offable.

I went back to what had worked well for me for one very short period of my life: when my boys were little, I designated Tuesday as Bathroom Cleaning Day and Thursday as Laundry Day.

Something crazy happened. My bathrooms were clean most of the time, and we had clean clothes to wear every day.

Shocker, right?

This strategy worked well, but I stopped doing it.

Why do I stop doing something that is working?

I have two theories. First, life happened, and this routine fizzled. I probably missed every Tuesday for a month because other things kept coming up. Second, I was used to all my methods fizzling. I expected them to fizzle. I waited for the fizzle. I didn't fight for this one to *not* fizzle.

Anyway, I decided to give the certain-days-for-certain-cleaning-tasks thing another try. I chose tasks that seemed momentous but that I knew I should probably do every week. I didn't research "What big cleaning tasks should I do every week?" I simply tried to think of the big stuff that had to be done in the week before I had a party. I could adjust later, but I needed to start.

I made Monday Laundry Day. In the first four months of deslobifying, I'd tried so hard to make laundry a daily task. I'd failed again and again.

Tuesdays I cleaned bathrooms. Wednesdays I ran errands and grocery shopped, Thursdays I mopped the kitchen, and Fridays I dusted and vacuumed.

My made-up routine worked.

At first it worked because I was doing those things. Bathrooms were clean because I cleaned them. The floor was mopped because I mopped it.

Profound, right? It wasn't. It was just a matter of making those things happen. As I gave this new-to-me "method" of assigning certain tasks to certain days a try, I began to understand *why* it worked well for me. When all my big cleaning was inspiration-dependent, the length between cleanings was a vague memory, a nagging feeling, and doing the task again depended on noticing. With Slob Vision, I'm not good at noticing. By the time I noticed the floor needed to be mopped, the floor *really* needed to be mopped, and mopping was an urgent, huge task.

When I knew Thursday was Mopping Day, I realized I needed to mop every time Thursday came around. Noticing was random, but Thursdays aren't. They happen every week.

Not that I mop every Thursday. Mopping on Thursday is the goal, but life happens. But instead of a nagging feeling that I should probably be mopping, I don't have to think about it. When I realize I've missed previous Thursdays, I am naturally more aware of how long it actually has been since the last time I mopped.

So I mop.

Never-ending cleaning tasks are nagging feelings. I despise nagging feelings. But nagging feelings go away when I have a plan, and the only thing I need for this plan is an awareness of the day of the week. Usually, even *I* am aware of that.

And the beauty of Thursday being Mopping Day is that Friday through Wednesday *aren't* mopping days. I don't have to think about mopping unless it's Thursday. I don't have to let dirty toilets nag at me on Fridays.

Not that the toilets don't ever get a special kind of dirty on Fridays. With a family of five, toilets get dirty on their own schedule. Stomach viruses don't wait until Monday night. But when I'm keeping up with my weekly cleaning tasks, I only have to deal with the special circumstances, not the special circumstances on top of who-knows-how-long's worth of a dirty bathroom. I can deal with the mess, and then I'm done until next Tuesday.

It's freeing, and it works.

But don't start with weekly cleaning tasks. Start with doing the dishes. I know the big stuff is more glamorous and has a bigger wow factor. I get that, but you're after traction. Doing this out of order won't bring the traction you so desperately want.

Daily tasks make a huge impact. They keep a house under control. Big cleaning tasks feel like the thing, but daily stuff is the thing.

Daily tasks make the weekly stuff possible. Really.

If your house is a wreck and you decide to clean bathrooms, what will that involve? For me, pre-blog, cleaning the bathroom involved picking up dirty laundry off the floor, putting away toothbrushes and hairbrushes, and throwing away three empty tubes of toothpaste. I had to do those things before I could clean the bathroom, so that felt like part of cleaning the bathroom. My idea of how long it took to clean bathrooms was severely warped. As someone whose concept of time is warped anyway, this isn't good.

When I check bathrooms for clutter every day (habit 3 in "28 Days to Hope for Your Home"), I get to *just* clean the bathroom, so I am more willing to do it.

If you don't believe me, time yourself cleaning the bathroom. Then time yourself again on a week when you're rocking the daily tasks.

A big reason why cleaning my house was a daunting and overwhelming task was I didn't understand cleaning and decluttering are not the same thing. I didn't understand because, without daily tasks, they *were* the same thing. I *did* have to get rid of the layer of clutter before I could clean. Just like I didn't know how long it took to do the dishes, I didn't know how long it took to clean the bathroom without first having to deal with what should have already been done.

> A big reason why cleaning my house was a daunting and overwhelming task was I didn't understand cleaning and decluttering are not the same thing.

But what if you don't have time each day for a big task? What if you work twelve-hour shifts and there's no consistency to your weeks? Do what works for you. Try different ways until you find one that works, but keep up with the daily tasks while you're figuring it out. Unfortunately, the daily tasks have to be done no matter how crazy life gets.

Maybe you'll have a Cleaning Day where you do all the major cleaning tasks on Saturday. Maybe you'll clean bathrooms on the first and third Saturdays and dust, vacuum, and mop on the second and fourth.

Did you notice I didn't mention laundry in this alternate, I-can't-assign-a-day scenario? Laundry needs to be a weekly task no matter how unique your schedule, for multiple reasons. Laundry gets its very own chapter, and that chapter is coming right up.

Proof It's Not Just Me

"Having the weekly cleaning tasks helps me keep on track with changing our bed sheets since we've designated Monday as bedding day. The bathrooms do much better, too, with having the task assigned to one day a week."

—Elizabeth M.

"Learning about Slob Vision was such an 'aha!' moment for me. I, too, do not see mess in increments. Things are either completely clean or a total disaster. I started a manageable daily routine that I have kept up, and my weekly deep clean now takes a Saturday morning. I force myself to take time each day to look around and put things back in order. I actually feel like at any moment I can have guests over without having to worry."

—Anonymous

II

Laundry Conquered. Yes, Really.

Fantasy: If I do one load every single day, I'll never have huge piles of dirty laundry!

Reality: I start a load but forget to come back and finish it. I rewash the same souring load again and again, while the rest of my dirty clothes pile higher and higher.

Do you know what that is a picture of? Monday's dirty clothes. Do you know what today is? Tuesday. (It's Tuesday while I'm writing this chapter. I have no idea which day you're reading this.)

Do you remember what Monday is in my house? Laundry Day. We wash, dry, and put away all the clothes that are dirty on Monday morning.

After a day spent washing a week's worth of clothes for five people, the sight of more, newly dirtied laundry could feel like a slap in the face. At one time in my life, it did. Laundry was a never-ending story, but not the good kind. I felt like I was drowning. I'd push my way to the surface, gulp the air, but more dirty laundry would suddenly appear, wrapping around my ankle and pulling me back down.

I couldn't get away from laundry. I couldn't get ahead.

I don't know about your family's quirks, but mine has this weird obsession with wearing clothes. Like, every single day.

You know by now that in the early days of my deslobification process, I added a new nonnegotiable task every week. Technically, I added a new task *almost* every week. One thing kept messing me up. Laundry. One week's focus on laundry didn't work, so I made it my focus for another week. And then another.

I never succeeded at making laundry a daily task in my home.

Laundry's different from doing dishes. You have to remember. Remembering isn't my strongpoint.

I can realize I need to wash dishes and . . . *go wash dishes*. Once they're done, I go on with my life. I love going on with my life. I love being done.

Laundry was never over when I tried it as a daily task.

I can get a bee in my bonnet about laundry and decide I'm going to change forever and never struggle with this dumb task again. I gather the most necessary items (undies, socks, and such), stick them in the washing machine, measure the detergent, and push the buttons.

And then I have to wait. I can't do another thing with that load of clothes until the washing machine has done its job.

I could sit in a chair and watch the movement of the knob or the ticking of the time, ready to pounce when the load is done. But no sane person is going to do that (and I'm not going to do it either).

When the physical actions required to complete a task have gaping time holes of thirty minutes or more in between, I have a problem. Because thirty minutes is just enough time for me to lose all memory of this wild idea I had about getting laundry under control once and for all.

I can't fit laundry into an awkward pause. I can fit the *first* part into these little spaces, but who knows where my brain or my body will be when it's time to switch to the dryer.

When "Laundry!" pops into my brain, I can start, *but I can't finish.*

Finishing is my problem in the first place, so things that don't allow finishing are a special form of slob torture.

I know so many of the world's most organized people do one load of laundry a day. I tried. I really, really tried.

I tried finding reminder moments in my day. Starting the washing machine before I went to bed and moving clothes to the dryer as soon as I got up the next morning seemed logical. I might remember before bed, but when I opened the lid, I found the previous night's load still sitting in the washing machine. I'd forgotten to move it. Now last night's load was stinky and had to be washed again. The new load would have to wait.

The next night, I found that same blankety-blank load, and I had to wash it a third time.

Blergh.

I looked for a trigger in the morning to help me remember to switch over the load. Empty the dishwasher and switch over the laundry. That sounded doable.

But while I could fit unloading the dishwasher into a five-minute pause between making lunches and taking kids to school, I could rarely fit unloading the dishwasher *and* switching over the laundry—if it actually occurred to me to try.

I tried setting the alarm on my phone. Did you know the alarm goes off even if your phone is on silent? Even if you're in an ultraquiet situation where people give the stink-eye to someone whose phone starts playing an obnoxious tune? It does. I know this. In your frantic embarrassment, you turn off the alarm and never think to turn it on again.

I know this too.

I even tried leaving the door of our laundry room open so it would block our bedroom exit and I would *physically* run into the door when I got up in the morning. Except Hubby usually gets up before I do. He didn't like this idea.

My point is this: I tried. I simply could not make a daily habit of this task that required three separate rememberings every single day. I could remember to start the process because the dirty clothes were in front of my face. I just couldn't remember to take them out of either the washer or the dryer once they were closed up inside and totally invisible.

But when I started working on a way to tackle the big, stop-life-for-a-moment-while-I-scrub-this-toilet stuff and assigned major tasks to days of the week, I put laundry in the rotation.

> Like no other housekeeping strategy has ever worked for me, Laundry Day worked perfectly and consistently—and kept on working. Six years later, Laundry Day still works.

It worked. Like no other housekeeping strategy has ever worked for me, Laundry Day worked perfectly and consistently—and kept on working. Six years later, Laundry Day still works.

If the thought of a Laundry Day overwhelms you, let me explain how and why it works for me.

We've established that I like projects—tasks with a beginning, a middle, and an end. Laundry Day means laundry is a project, and as a project, it's all the things I love.

Not that I love laundry, because . . . stinky socks. But I love the way this task works for me.

On Mondays, laundry is my focus. I've gone on and on (and on) about how focus is the problem and I can't remember to change over the load. I can't remember to change over *one load every single day*, but I do remember when laundry is my entire focus for the day. I don't have to worry about cleaning bathrooms or dusting the living room because Monday is all about laundry. Monday is *only* about laundry.

I'm racing. I have a goal and a finish line.

Here's how the day goes:

Step 1: Sort the clothes. All the dirty laundry in the entire house. For real.

We do this on Sunday night. Wait. You thought Monday was my Laundry Day? It is. But we sort on Sunday night to be ready for Monday.

My family gets so excited when I yell, "Bring me your dirty clothes!" (If, by *excited*, you mean groaning and moaning and grumbling, then yes, they're excited.)

We sort the dirty clothes into piles. There are people in the world who are antisorting. Yay for them. I can't do it, and I don't need to with this method. Abandoning sorting might make sense if you're doing one load a day, but for us, with five people who wear clothes every single day, we usually end up with two loads of darks, one load of lights, one load of whites, and one load of jeans and dark towels. And usually one more load that alternates between sheets or other randomness.

Skeptical? That's only five or six loads. Are you thinking there's no way your family would only have five loads? Maybe you wouldn't. But my guess (since you didn't skip this chapter, thinking, *Laundry? What kind of loser struggles with laundry? It's so eeaassssy!*) is you might not have a true understanding of how many loads of laundry your family creates in one week.

I didn't. I had zero concept of one week's worth of laundry until my second laundry day. The truth didn't sink in until week three or four.

Here's what I knew: When I got it in my head to do *all* the laundry and sorted it all, there were piles of dirty clothes down the hallway and covering the floor of the living room. There were *so* many clothes.

I'd do as much as I could, piling the clean stuff on the couch until it toppled over and then piling more on the dining room table. I'd get mad at my family when they kept wearing the clothes I'd just washed, and then I'd add the dirty-again clothes to the piles I hadn't finished yet. The piles would grow and grow and never go away.

The first Laundry Day is no indication of how Laundry Day will work in your house.

If you are behind on laundry, you won't wash one week's worth of clothes. You will wash all the clothes you never washed when you were only doing emergency loads of socks and undies and clothes people needed for school and work.

The first Laundry Day will include the extra clothes you bought because you didn't think you had enough, because you were always running out of clean ones. The first Laundry Day will include the clothes your kids outgrew last year, which have been sitting at the bottom of the laundry pile because you knew they didn't fit so there was no point in washing them. Who has time to wash things to donate when you're behind on the clothes your family needs right now?

Worst of all, if you're behind, the first Laundry Day won't take one day. It might take all week.

But here is the key to stopping the endless cycle:

Once all the laundry in the house has been sorted into piles, any new dirty laundry goes in the hamper (or wherever you throw your dirty laundry).

Do not add newly dirtied clothes to the sorted piles. The newly dirtied clothes are next week's laundry.

Don't worry about next week's laundry. Your only concern is this week's laundry, and this week's laundry is already in piles, waiting to go through the washer and dryer.

Keep trudging through. Wash all of this accumulated dirty laundry and tackle it as a project. It has an end. By definition, if you can get through all of these piles before next week's Laundry Day, you'll have won.

But (and this is important) even if you finish Laundry Day Number One on Saturday at midnight after starting it the previous Monday, the next Monday (the one that's less than 48 hours away) is your next Laundry Day. Even though you don't want to look at another dirty sock ever again.

Start over. Sort every piece of dirty laundry in the house into piles. Again.

Do you see a difference? You should. A fairly significant, visible difference.

This is one week's worth of laundry. For real. You have to do it today, because *next* week, the beauty of Laundry Day will finally sink in.

The magic happens on the third Laundry Day. You washed and dried a ridiculous number of loads on the first Laundry Day. On the second one, you're mad at me for saying you need to start again with another Laundry Day because you're sick to death of laundry. You finally finished those fifty ba-jillion loads, and you deserve a break.

But on the third Laundry Day, you've experienced the much-coveted break. You did the second Laundry Day, and it only took a day (or so). Not the entire week like the first one did.

And then you were done. You lived an entire week being done with laundry. You didn't worry about having clean undies; you just reached into the drawer (or, let's be honest, dug through the pile on the couch) and grabbed a pair.

> Laundry Day is worth my time because there's such a thing as being done with laundry, contrary to what Internet memes and commiserating housewives claim.

You saw the hamper getting fuller and fuller, and the growing laundry pile didn't nag at your soul.

That's next Laundry Day's laundry.

You experienced six whole days that weren't Laundry Day. Those six nagging-feeling-free days make you strangely excited for the next Laundry Day.

Laundry Day is worth my time because there's such a thing as being done with laundry, contrary to what Internet memes and commiserating housewives claim.

Laundry Day lets me make laundry a project. It gives this never-ending task a beginning, a middle, and an end. And it lets me be done, completely finished, for six days in a row.

Wow. I rambled on for a long time after stating that step 1 is sorting. Let's move on.

Step 2: Wash the first load of clothes. I usually put the first load in on Sunday night.

Step 3: When the washing machine finishes, put those clothes in the dryer and then put another load of dirty clothes in the washing machine.

Step 4: When the dryer finishes, fold clothes as you take them out of the dryer and put them in their proper drawers and closets throughout the house immediately. Move wet clothes from the washing machine into the dryer, start it, and put the next load of dirty clothes in the washing machine and start it.

Step 5: Repeat steps 3 and 4 until every pile is gone.

So simple, right?

12

A Whole 'Nuther Chapter on Laundry (Answering Your Many Objections)

Fantasy: I have an amazing ability to think through situations. I can identify superfluous actions better than the average person.

Reality: While I love the word *superfluous*, I tend to make things harder than they need to be by coming up with reasons not to do what needs to be done.

Objection #1: Folding Right Out of the Dryer Is Dumb

Now I'll go back and address the things you audibly scoffed at in the last chapter.

Let's start with step 4. The part where I (rudely and bossily and like a total know-it-all) told you to fold clothes as you take them out of the dryer and then put them away immediately.

First of all, you don't have to do that for Laundry Day to have a huge impact on your home. For years after I started Laundry Day, I didn't. I resisted the fold-it-right-out-of-the-dryer-and-put-it-away-immediately thing with every fiber of my being. I argued (in my head and out loud to anyone who cared) that I just needed to get this stuff through the cycle. I could fold and put them away any time, but I needed to get the next load into the washer as quickly as possible because the time clothes spend in the washing machine is the one thing I *can't* control.

Folding immediately wouldn't be an efficient use of my time, and I loved (the idea of) being efficient!

I was wrong.

You may have noticed a common theme in this book. Any time I over-logicalize a task to the point where I convince myself that stopping at a halfway place makes sense, it doesn't end well.

Even if dumping clean clothing on the love seat so I can get a new load in the washer and dryer more quickly seems totally efficient to my Slob Brain, it's not.

It didn't work. My argument that it should work was completely logical, but it *didn't* work.

> I have no interest in what *should* work. I care about only what *does* work.

I have no interest in what *should* work. I care about only what *does* work.

I tried. I designated my bed or the kitchen table as my Clean Laundry Dumping Ground, thinking I'd be forced to fold it before I went to bed or served dinner.

I thought wrong.

These places were halfway points, and halfway points are Procrastination Stations. Procrastination breeds more procrastination. Once I've put off folding and putting away so I can move more loads through the washer and dryer, I've set myself up to continue on with my day without ever thinking to go back to that pile like I totally thought I would. I repeat this procrastinating-with-the-best-of-intentions, and the pile grows.

No amount of surprise at seeing clothes piled high on my bed makes me fold them before I go to sleep. I'd prefer to move them, armful by armful, into the living room. Temporarily. I'm really tired. *I've been doing laundry all day.*

When I finally gave up the fight and tried the fold-it-right-out-of-the-dryer method, something crazy happened. I was done.

Like, done for real.

As each load comes out of my dryer, I go against my efficiency instinct and fold the clothes immediately. I place them in stacks on top of the washing machine and the opened dryer door. If the stacks need more space than I have, I put away what is already folded and come back to finish.

This means I sometimes make *two different trips* to the same place. That's, like, the complete *opposite* of efficiency.

And yet, good things happen. Laundry disappears.

This phenomenon was honestly a little freaky at first. With each load I finished, the volume of clothing in my house seemed to shrink. I started the day with piles of dirty laundry on the floor. But as the day went on, they disappeared into thin air. Technically, they were in their proper drawers and closets. But visually, they were *gone*. Put away. Out of my vision, conscious or unconscious. Out of my brain, not taking up a bit of mental energy on my subconscious to-do list.

It's really kind of freaky.

But you don't have to do that. Really.

I encourage you to fold laundry right out of the dryer because it changed everything (or at least everything laundry-related) for me, but you don't have to. Pile your clean laundry on the couch. Find a mental trick (or at least try a few) to make yourself fold clothes before you go to bed. Use folding as an excuse to watch your favorite show.

Even if you don't do Laundry Day exactly the way I do, it will rock your world in a very good way.

Objection #2: My Laundry Day Couldn't Possibly Look Like Yours

I get it. The idea of Laundry Day is overwhelming. When there's a task you hate doing anyway, the thought of spending an entire day doing it (or an entire week that first time) is, honestly, crazy. Crazy enough to make you think of all the reasons it could never work in order to justify not giving Laundry Day a try.

I was the queen of logical justifications, of talking myself out of a tried and proven way of doing something so I wouldn't have to try it.

The fact is, your Mondays, your weeks, your home, your life situation don't look exactly like mine. I get that. There's an entire chapter coming up about that very issue.

As a writer, I work at home, and I can choose a weekday Laundry Day. Maybe your Laundry Day will have to be Saturday.

But my Mondays don't look the same every single week, and neither will your Saturdays. I'm not always home on Mondays, and you won't always be home on Saturdays. I'm sometimes gone from 7:00 a.m. to 6:00 p.m. Instead of throwing this routine out the window, I do my best to make the process work. Once laundry is truly under control (by the third or fourth Laundry Day), it's not even that difficult to adjust.

Knowing I'll be gone the next day, I'm motivated to get a second load in the washing machine before I go to bed on Sunday night. Then, in the hustle of an out-of-routine morning, I'm determined to immediately get Sunday night's load into the dryer the minute I get up and another load into the washing machine. I feel like I'm rocking it if I can get *that* load into the dryer and another into the washer before I leave for the day. Because Laundry Day has a finish line, it's like a race.

I get home on Monday evening and switch out another load.

Were you counting? That was five loads, which is usually the number of loads I do each week. Even when I had a smaller washing machine and did seven loads each week, this kind of focus, this knowing *today* is the day to do laundry, helped me get it done. This might be a week when I don't fold straight out of the dryer, but our clothes are clean.

Sometimes, I just get behind. Laundry Day stretches into Tuesday or Wednesday. That's okay, because I'm still *finishing* Laundry Day. There's still an end in sight. I'm just taking a little longer to finish this project of washing all our dirty clothes from last week.

If you work a full-time job outside your home and resent terribly the idea of spending your Saturday washing clothes (when you also need to shop and spend time with your kids and do everything else), work toward the goal of a Laundry Day that looks like my Monday-when-I'm-gone-from-sunup-to-sundown version. This might mean you have to first spend a few Saturdays doing the horrible first and second Laundry Days, but you probably already had to do those Laundry Weekends occasionally just to survive. Or head to the Laundromat to get caught up so you can start out with a true one-week's-worth of laundry.

Do whatever you have to do to make it work in your home.

Imperfection is welcome. Laundry Day is a thing, and you can do that thing however you want to do it, *if* you want to do it. If laundry isn't a problem for you, keep doing what you're doing. But if you are forever frustrated by your inability to keep laundry under control, give Laundry Day a try. It might work for you too.

Maybe your Laundry Day will look different from mine. Maybe you have twelve kids, and Mondays, Wednesdays, and Fridays need to all be Laundry Days. That would work. Or maybe you have a septic tank and can't do five or six loads in one day because it would overload the system. Experiment. See what works. Do kid laundry one day and adult another. Just find a way to put an end to this never-ending task. Make a plan that includes an ending point.

> Do whatever you have to do to make it work in your home.

You may try Laundry Day and find out it doesn't work for you, and that's fine. But if you're anything like me and can come up with doozie excuses that don't actually play out in life the way they do in your head, you need to try it before you decide Laundry Day isn't for you.

A Few More Things That Come Up When People Talk About Laundry

When do you wash sheets? Or random items like blankets or tablecloths that don't fit in with a normal Laundry Day and need their own load?

One of the beautiful things about being *done* with laundry every week is that my washing machine is totally free, both physically and psychologically, six(ish) days each week.

So when the dog pukes on my daughter's blanket, I can stick the blanket straight into the washing machine. I don't have to first rewash the load that's been getting stinky for the past two days. I don't have to feel guilty that I'm running an undie-free load because we have plenty of clean undies in our drawers. I can change all the sheets on Friday and run two loads. I can throw dirty kitchen towels into the open washer to wait for Laundry Day. I'm free, and my washing machine is free, and I can do what I need to do when I need to do it.

There's one last thing. You (probably) don't need a new washing machine. As long as your machine gets clothes clean, you can do this. The answer to your laundry problems isn't a bigger-capacity machine or a jingle that signals the end of a load. These things are nice, but I didn't have them until I'd been making Laundry Day work for four whole years. To get laundry under control, you need a routine. All the features and gadgets in the world won't make a difference without a routine.

Unfortunately.

. . . .

Proof It's Not Just Me

"I'm so glad I learned about having a single weekly laundry day. It seemed I was never finished doing laundry, and remembering to switch loads over was very hit-or-miss, more often miss than hit if I'm being completely honest with myself. Now it is such a relief to have all the laundry done and not have to face that particular task for an entire week. Such a blessing to our home!"

—Alicia G.

"I was reluctant to try Laundry Day—the backup was never so bad—but I moved to a very small apartment and have to lug all my laundry to the Laundromat. . . . . The first day was the worst (nine loads of laundry to drag all that way!), but since then having a dedicated laundry day helps me organize my schedule. I have been really loving the routine: go, wash, play on playground with toddler, dry, come home, sort/fold. Carving out space to take care of the whole chore all at once actually makes it a much less daunting chore."

—Rachel R.

"My laundry had taken over the basement. I heard about Laundry Day on your podcast. I thought that would not work for me. One load every day would be better. But I've tried that before and clothes sit in the washer needing a vinegar rewash, so I gave in and tried. Now, Monday is my laundry day. I start on Sunday night and end on Tuesday morning. I don't have to think about laundry the rest of the week! I fold and sort right from the dryer and I put tons of stuff straight from the dryer to the donate bag! I can see a difference and more importantly, I found a system that is not overwhelming."

—Anonymous

13

Get Dinner on the Table

Fantasy: I love to cook. I enjoy spending time in the kitchen, cooking food from scratch, serving meals my family loves, and gathering around the table so we can invest in one another's lives.

Reality: I love to cook, but there might be three days a year when I have an entire hour to devote to a single meal. I'm determined to eat together as a family, but fitting that into our schedule usually means I have less than thirty minutes to spend in the kitchen.

I've covered the basics you need in order to avoid a disastrous kitchen, smelly bathrooms, and empty sock drawers. But there's another daily task that will send you into panic mode every evening at five o'clock if you don't have a strategy in place.

Meal planning.

Or, to put it more realistically, making sure your family doesn't starve.

Before I move out of this section on habits and daily tasks, I'm sharing the basics of my meal-planning strategies. Eating is a daily task. For most people, it's a three-times-a-day daily task. When other people depend on you to feed them, it can also be a very stressful task.

Entire books exist on this subject, but I'm giving meal planning one chapter. I'm sharing only my best tricks, but, like everything else in the area of home management, a few good tricks can make a big impact.

When my husband and I were newlyweds, we had one car and drove to work together. Most nights, we decided what we were going to have for dinner as we drove home. About twice a week (not counting every single weekend meal), we'd stop somewhere so I wouldn't have to cook.

In my mind, this was acceptable because it was only the two of us and I was working full time. I justified eating out because I was tired and we technically had the money to do it. But on those trips home, feeling a twinge of guilt every time I decided not to cook, I dreamed of the day when I would be . . . a stay-at-home mom.

As a stay-at-home mom, home-cooked meals would happen. Naturally. And *my* home-cooked meals would be made completely from scratch. I even priced wheat grinders on the Internet. That's how far I planned to take this "from scratch" dream of mine.

Why not? I was going to be a *stay-at-home mom*. What else would I have to do?

One of those drives home sticks out in my memory. I even remember the specific stoplight where my husband and I waited as this conversation unfolded. I said (in an ultradreamy tone) something along the lines of "Just think. Once we have kids, we'll never eat processed cheese again!"

My daydream was abruptly interrupted by my husband's gasp of horror. "What? Why not?"

"I'll make everything from scratch. We won't *need* convenience foods!"

His excitement didn't mirror mine.

He grew up eating processed cheese loaf and loved it. I like it, too, but easy-melt cheese wasn't part of my idealistic view of how I was going to cook once I had all the time in the world available for cooking.

And then we actually had kids. I'm sure you can guess what happened. The baby who never cried in my daydreams cried nonstop the minute I walked into the kitchen. Then he had a little brother. The little brother cried, too, while the big brother pulled everything out of the cabinets. Things weren't going the way I expected.

But eating dinner together every night wasn't optional. Dusting was optional; cooking wasn't. I'm loosey-goosey on some things and driven/stubborn/unstoppable on others. Over time, I figured out the most essential things I needed to do to get dinner on the table on a nightly basis, no matter how crazy our schedule or how loud the baby's cries.

A Plan and a List

Make a list. Buy a pretty notebook or grab a torn envelope off the kitchen table. Jot down four or five meals you can eat over the next week. Think through each meal (read the recipes if you're into using actual recipes, which I'm not) and check your fridge, freezer, and cabinets to see what you have and don't have. Write down what you need before you head to the store.

If you have a smartphone, stick the envelope-list on your fridge and take a picture of it. That way, your list will be in two places. You can look at the list on the fridge when it's time to start dinner each night, and you can use the picture of the list while you're at the store.

A plan reduces the need for creativity and problem-solving during difficult hours when babies are crying and football practices are ending. It's a pre-made decision.

A list increases the likelihood you'll have what you need to make those meals.

> A plan reduces the need for creativity and problem-solving during difficult hours when babies are crying and football practices are ending.

When I don't plan or make a list, I end up reaching into the fridge for the final ingredient (for the meal that's already in progress) only to realize I don't have it.

A list also saves money. I spend significantly more money when I wander through the store grabbing things I think might be good for putting meals together. A list is important.

81

Stock Up

Smart shoppers stock up on the basics when they're on sale. This isn't a book about smart shopping, but stocking up on basics is a good thing for a scatterbrained mama as well. I can tell you (and tell myself) how important it is to always have a list and a plan, but we all know that isn't going to happen every single week. Even when life gets crazy and I don't make it to the store, we still need to eat.

Here's how stocking up on food works: Start paying attention to how much you are paying for things you buy consistently. Look at the front page of your grocery store's sales flyer. The very best deals will be on the front page. When something you buy consistently (and that will last awhile because it can be frozen or stored in the pantry) is on sale for less than you usually pay, buy a few extra. If I have meat and frozen vegetables in the freezer and pasta in the pantry, I can make a basic meal no matter how crazy my week.

Use Your Project Brain for Good

As a Project Person, the idea of freezer cooking appealed to me. I loved the thought of spending one weekend cooking and having meals prepared for a month.

But I never actually did it.

I never got around to the huge shopping trip or the full day of cooking. But after hearing about the concept, I did start doubling some of our favorite meals, such as chicken tortilla soup or spinach lasagna, and freezing the extra.

Once I experienced the joy of eating a home-cooked meal without spending time or energy in the kitchen, I started looking for more ways to use my freezer to make life easier.

When I grilled chicken breasts, I grilled extra and froze them. When I browned ground beef, I browned extra and froze it. When I made meatballs, I baked extra.

Every time I made chicken fajitas or tacos or spaghetti or chili without first thawing the meat, cooking it, and cleaning up the greasy mess, I was inspired to precook more the next time.

My whole view of meal prep started changing. The more often I had already-cooked chicken in the freezer, the more easily I could get dinner on the table quickly, no matter how needy a teething baby might be.

As a Project Person, I like to work hard on things that make life easier. This doesn't work for dirty dishes, but it works well for this kind of freezer cooking. I call it "this kind of" because when many people think about freezer meals, they don't think of this. They think about casseroles. I was so confused when my mother-in-law asked me what kinds of casseroles I'd been making before our third child was born. I didn't remember the conversation she said we'd had until I realized she was asking about food I'd prepared ahead and frozen. She assumed frozen meals were casseroles. I like casseroles but haven't ever done well freezing them. I can't remember to thaw.

Besides, my visions of being an inventive cook hadn't died completely. I didn't want to make casseroles because they seemed so confining. What if I wasn't in the *mood* for that particular combination on the day we needed to eat it?

Precooking *ingredients* works for me. If an ingredient can be frozen, I cook more than I need for the recipe I'm already making. If I make marinara sauce from scratch, I triple it. If I make a roast, I make enough for four meals. If I make rice, I boil the entire package. If we have a big breakfast on Saturday morning, cooking extra sausage means we have it on weekday mornings too. Making extra adds very little time to the meal I'm making anyway, but it saves huge amounts of time in the future.

What is the most time-consuming step of your family's favorite meals? Most likely, it's cooking the meat. If that step (and the mess involved) were already done, how much more likely would you be to cook? My guess is *way*. As in, *way more likely*.

Idealist mamas know they need to cook. They know all the facts about how kids are more likely to be successful if they eat dinner around the table with their families on a regular basis. (If you didn't know that, it's true.) They know cooking at home is key to good health and staying within budget.

This kind of freezer cooking significantly increases the likelihood that your family will eat home-cooked food.

. . . .

Proof It's Not Just Me

"I use the slow cooker at least twice a week. If the recipe calls for browning the meat first (as it often does), instead of doing that in the morning, I now brown it over the weekend and freeze until I'm making that recipe. It makes it so much easier to throw everything in the slow cooker in the morning!"

—April M.

"Once a month, I brown several dozen pounds of ground beef and chicken breasts in my Crock-Pot, shred or cut up the chicken, and put the beef or chicken in individual, portion-sized baggies. Not only does the meat seem to thaw quicker, but it makes dinner so much quicker and easier."

—Julie W.

"We love this trick! We preseason some ground beef for taco meat or Mexican casseroles; chicken can go straight into a soup, and ground beef can go directly into a dish in the oven or stove top without worrying about added grease, because it has already been cooked and drained! Depending on the meal, there is generally no need to let it thaw before adding it to a dish, so when I am behind in my dinner prep, it is a big time-saver."

—Jena S.

"I precook ground beef and freeze in one-pound bags for pasta sauce, chili, or tacos. So nice to only make the grease mess once. I've also started cooking a Crock-Pot full of shredded chicken at the beginning of the week to use in recipes throughout the week."

—Meghan H.

"After thirty-six years of marriage and making meals, I have found the joy of precooking meat! It has been the #1 game changer for us. I use the method of cooking a lot of chicken at once and shredding it. I package it in two-cup portions, and it is perfect for so many meals. I would offer this advice of precooking meat to any newlywed or new mother as the best time-saver method for clean eating at home!"

—Beth R.

Part 3

Decluttering:
The Down-and-Dirty
Truth About All Your Stuff

14

How Decluttering and Routines Are Codependent

Fantasy: I need to get this house decluttered. Then it will make sense to start doing daily tasks.

Reality: If I wait until I'm "done" decluttering, I'll be waiting forever.

Strange things happen when nonnegotiable tasks become the daily norm. Time expands. It's bizarre, really.

We've established that daily dishwashing takes significantly less time than washing the dishes every few days. It's irritating, but true. It's Dishes Math. Before this routine, I rarely thought I had free time to tackle decluttering projects, even on days when I didn't wash a single dish. But on a day when dishes are done, *all the way done*, in less than fifteen little ol' minutes, I have finished something visible, and the day is just beginning. One visible accomplishment inspires me to do more.

When housecleaning always started with the kitchen and the kitchen took hours, I rarely moved to the rest of the house. But with the kitchen clean in so much less time, I can move on to other things.

I needed to declutter. In the same way dirty dishes formed piles in my kitchen, random stuff formed piles everywhere else.

I loved stuff, and I had a lot of it. If something was cheap or free, if I liked it or imagined I might use it one day, I never asked "Why?" I asked "Why not?" and brought it home. All the stuff blended together and overwhelmed me.

Small, visible accomplishments clear my Slob Vision. The absence of dirty dishes on the kitchen counter opens my eyes. I see two empty cooking spray cans sitting next to the one that's full. In an otherwise clean kitchen, the empty cans are visibly out of place, so I pitch them.

This creates another visible improvement, and I'm inspired to keep going. I decide to declutter my kitchen cabinets. I have some time, since the dishes are already done.

Not only do routines magically free up time for decluttering, they show me what to declutter, and this removes decluttering angst. I know all about decluttering angst. As the queen of what-if scenarios, I can come up with a logical reason to keep almost any item I pull out of a pile.

The biggest problem was that, many times, I was right. My what-if scenarios *did* come true.

What if we run out of clean plates? What if someone stops by and we can't offer a drink because all our glasses are dirty? What if we don't have clean underwear on a random Thursday? What if I need to scribble a cryptic note so Hubby will know I've been kidnapped? Won't I be glad I kept that scrap of paper?

I've never needed to scribble clues for a search party, but we did run out of clean plates on a regular basis. The threat of going commando loomed like a dark cloud on any given day.

I needed more plates, more cups, and a jumbo pack of paper products just to be safe. Just in case. Even though those dishes couldn't possibly fit into my cabinets if they all happened to be clean at the same time.

But once I had a routine, my eyes were opened to reality. What-if scenarios settled down in my overactive imagination. I started trusting myself to do the dishes and knowing we had enough.

I understood my need to declutter because I experienced (daily, not as a freakish, once-in-a-lifetime thing) how difficult it was to fit plates into my cabinet when they all were clean at the same time. I knew I could survive with fewer plates because some were never used. They never left the cabinet.

After weeks of clean dishes, I realized I was choosing the same plates over and over.

I hadn't known which plates were my favorites because I'd never had a choice.

Once I could trust myself to have clean dishes available almost every night at dinnertime, getting rid of the ones we didn't need was easy.

We liked the ones I stuck in the dishwasher every night. I stuck them in the dishwasher every night because we used them every night. We used them every night because they were always clean.

I finally stopped buying plates. Constantly running out of plates meant I always had a nagging feeling we didn't have enough. I'd buy more and then could wait longer before doing the dishes. Since I waited longer, washing dishes required more time. And I'd get more overwhelmed.

And buy more plates.

And wait longer.

And the piles would get bigger.

And I'd feel more overwhelmed.

It was a vicious cycle.

But the cycle works the other way too. Once the extra plates were gone, putting dishes away was easier. I didn't have to angle and shove and push the door closed. I even stopped buying paper plates. I didn't need them anymore.

> Once I could trust myself to have clean dishes available almost every night at dinnertime, getting rid of the ones we didn't need was easy.

This phenomenon happened with oh-so-many things.

Once upon a time, I didn't know clothing could be clutter. Clothing is *useful.* You need clothes.

Like dishes, I only saw the truth about clothing as clutter once laundry was under control. Pre-Laundry Day, I had no idea how many clothes we had or how many we needed. I just knew we were always running out of clothes, so I always thought we needed more.

So I bought more. With more clothes, I could wait longer before I *had* to do laundry, but by the time I had to do it, the piles were so high I was completely overwhelmed.

If you're overwhelmed, hear this: decluttering your clothing will be easy when Laundry Day becomes a routine.

On the third Laundry Day, I noticed I was washing the exact same clothes I washed the last Laundry Day. My kids were experiencing something they hadn't before. All their clothes were clean at the same time.

They had this new thing called *choices*.

They chose their favorites. As soon as the favorites were clean again, they wore them again, *because they were their favorites*.

As I put laundry away on the third Laundry Day, I saw which clothes weren't being chosen. For the first time ever, I knew which clothes were favorites and which ones were worn only if there wasn't another option. This made decluttering easy.

I learned through experience that even good, useful, fits-pretty-well clothing can be clutter. *Anything I have too much of, that consistently gets out of control simply because I have too much of it, is clutter.*

> Anything I have too much of, that consistently gets out of control simply because I have too much of it, is clutter.

I hoarded undies because I was scared of running out of clean underwear. Once I could count on having clean undies every day, I could relax my grip on the ridiculous excess I'd been keeping.

This is why I'm begging you to start with habits. Start your own deslobification process by solving the unsolvable daily problems that frustrate you in your home. Habits make decluttering easier, and decluttering makes it easier to maintain habits.

They're codependent.

Keeping up with daily habits is hard (seemingly impossible sometimes) when clutter is everywhere. But decluttering will make no lasting impact without daily habits in place. I know this. If I turned my head away from a finished decluttering project, it was a disaster again when I looked back at it.

I didn't know what happened. Now I know, and it's really about what *didn't* happen. Habits didn't happen.

. . . .

Proof It's Not Just Me

"Since dishes were not a main priority in my house (there were some weeks where my husband and I only did them once in the week!), it was crucial to have multiples of everything! Seriously, who needs four pizza cutters? Three strainers? . . . That third day, when every single dish was finally washed, I gave away two sets of pots and pans and a bunch of other duplicates I had taking up space. It feels so freeing to know that overflowing dishes are not consuming my kitchen, and neither is the abundance of unnecessary clean ones!"

—Tabitha J.

"I have always embraced having a large, cute wardrobe. I decided that 'cute wardrobe' meant a huge laundry pile in my room. I got rid of three-quarters of my clothes so my pile is much smaller and actually gets washed and put away each week. This is me embracing reality. Honestly, I only miss that one sweater . . ."

—P.D.

"My husband and I habitually waited until every dish in our cluttered cupboards was dirty, then dreaded (and often fought about) the giant pile, which couldn't be washed in a single sitting. I started decluttering the dishes . . . and found that I actually did keep them clean longer when I had fewer to go through! Also, even when every dish in the house was dirty, I wasn't stuck at the sink for an hour."

—Sara P.

15

Don't Get Organized

Fantasy: I need to figure out how to organize all this stuff.

Reality: I have too much stuff.

I f you're overwhelmed with stuff, getting started will be the hardest part of any decluttering project. I know. I was there. I promise you can do this.

Here's step 1: Don't get organized.

"Get organized!" doesn't need to be on your list.

I'm not an anti-organizationalist. But "getting organized" is no longer my goal when I tackle an out-of-control space.

It used to be. Organizing seemed like a great project, and I love projects. I'd think, I'd analyze, and I'd purchase organizing supplies. Bins, boxes, and baskets seemed like the perfect solution to my problem.

By the time I got home from the store, the excitement I felt about getting organized had waned. Fizzled. The big, clunky bag filled with lovely new containers was set aside and forgotten.

Not only had I successfully procrastinated, I had more *stuff* in my house than I did before I started organizing.

But even when I didn't fall into this must-buy-more-cute-organizing-stuff trap, I struggled.

Organizing is problem-solving. Problem-solving (especially when I've failed at exactly that over and over and over) is overwhelming. I stared. I analyzed. I devised strategies and thought of every possible way those strategies could fail.

> Organizing is problem-solving. Problem-solving (especially when I've failed at exactly that over and over and over) is overwhelming.

I felt pressure to solve the problem once and for all, in a way that would last through all of my family's future stages.

As I started my deslobification process, I was determined to avoid ways that had consistently failed me in the past. So even though I was sure "getting organized" was my goal, I had to change the way I did it. In the same way I went about developing habits, I started as small as I possibly could: I focused only on getting stuff out of our house.

A Little of My Clutter Story

I started my adult life with way too much stuff. Before my husband and I were married, we each lived on our own and had everything we needed for basic living. We also received a *lot* of wedding gifts. They filled the living room of our apartment when we returned from our honeymoon.

With my stuff, his stuff, and our new stuff, I knew we had three toasters, but I didn't get rid of the two we weren't using. I didn't think I needed to because we had an extra room in our apartment for the sole purpose of storing stuff. I thought keeping everything until we had a house was wiser, more frugal. Once we had a house, once we were settled, *then* we would decide what we needed. There's no reason to decide now when you can put off a decision for later.

I see so many things wrong with that mind-set now, but at the time, it was inarguably logical.

Why keep all that stuff? *Why not?*

When we moved into our house two years later, I purged a lot but held on to anything and everything that had any kind of potential for any possible future point in our lives. As an idealist, I love the word *potential*, and I couldn't bear to get rid of something that had it.

And then . . . I discovered garage sales. Soon after that, I discovered eBay. Not long after that, I put the two together.

On the surface, this was an amazing combination. I was spending quarters to buy other people's clutter, and I was selling it for dollars. As a stay-at-home mom, eBay was exciting. I'd never known of a way to make extra money while my babies napped.

But I bought faster than I sold, and my house became more and more cluttered with stuff I didn't even want for myself. When we moved to a new city, the main thing I looked for in a new house was an eBay room. An eBay room would be a dedicated space for all this random stuff I was bringing home, and it would solve all my problems. I got my eBay room, and I filled it up. The other rooms filled with my regular clutter.

As our family grew, I began to see the dark and scary side of our over-abundance of stuff. My kids' rooms were full of toys, but they couldn't play with them because they had no open space in which to play. The playroom was literally knee-deep in costumes and toys, and no one wanted to go in there.

And then one day, my mother brought each of my children a plant. She's a garden-club fanatic, and she chose a specific plant for each of my kids. The child who was least likely to water received the cactus, the nurturing one was given the plant that wouldn't die (as easily) from overwatering, and the kid who likes to show off got the one with lush, flowing leaves. She's an exceptional grammy. She told the kids she would enter their plants in a contest after a few months.

The kids were excited. A contest? Their very own plants? Ribbons? The idea sounded wonderful to them. My mother pulled a baker's rack out of her minivan and brought it into my house. The rack had three rows, perfectly sized to hold the plants. As she set up the shelf, tears sprang to my eyes, and I began to feel short of breath.

I recognized the shelf. My mother and I bought it for my college apartment. When I was pregnant with my first child, I painted it white and used it in his nursery.

I'd given the shelf to my mother about a year before. I had decluttered it.

My heart palpitated when I gave her that shelf. Decluttering something so completely and totally useful is physically painful for people like me. The idea of it coming back into my home was completely overwhelming. I imagined it piled with clutter. I saw myself knocking it over as I squeezed by, trying to avoid all the other clutter in my home.

> I wanted my children to grow up with fond memories of simple things that are big in the mind of a child. The overabundance of stuff in my home was keeping me from being the mother I'd always dreamed of being.

I fought the urge to cry, and my panic made me feel ashamed. I had a real, experience-based fear that one more thing entering my home (especially something that had already left once) was going to send me over the edge.

I wanted to be the mom who embraced plant-watering contests for her toddlers. I wanted my children to grow up with fond memories of simple things that are big in the mind of a child. The overabundance of stuff in my home was keeping me from being the mother I'd always dreamed of being.

I know a shelf and a cactus aren't life-changers, but moments when something small threatens to send me over the edge are. I had to change my cluttered ways, but the efforts I made to get organized hardly seemed to make a dent.

When I started the blog, I focused on decluttering but assumed I wasn't doing enough. I thought I was decluttering now so I could eventually solve my problems by organizing. But as I decluttered, my house improved. It became more livable, and I was less overwhelmed. As stuff left, peace came. It just took a while to realize what was happening.

One day, with the need for video content as my motivation for working on my house (an example of my brilliant blogging-as-accountability plan), I tackled my boys' messy room. I didn't have much time to work before I picked them up from school, but I needed to make a video.

> As stuff left, peace came.

I decided I would just declutter. Without enough time to "organize," I was just going to get rid of stuff they didn't need. In the video, I apologized in advance for not doing enough. For not actually organizing.

Something strange happened: once I removed the things that needed to be removed, the space felt organized.

I realized that was what I'd been doing. I'd been *just* decluttering. And *just* decluttering was enough.

I gave myself permission to stop worrying about getting organized. I simply focused on getting rid of clutter.

Back to Telling You What to Do

When a space is decluttered, that space is comparatively organized. If I remove the things we don't need, there's nothing getting in the way of things we do need. We can function in that space. We can use it. And isn't that the goal of organizing?

Decluttering is simply getting rid of stuff I don't need. Organizing is problem-solving. When you have too much stuff, the problem is overwhelming and feels unsolvable. Giving myself permission to just declutter gave me permission to get started. I didn't need a plan or a huge chunk of time.

I'm giving you the same permission. Amazing freedom comes with this separation of organizing and decluttering.

As I experienced this freedom, I kept decluttering. As I kept decluttering, I began to see the beauty of less.

Less

Just declutter is my plan, and *less* is my goal.

When we have less, the house stays under control. With fewer toys, the kids' floors stay cleaner longer because they don't have as many things to pull off the shelves and scatter across the carpet. With fewer pots and pans, the kitchen cabinets close easily.

With less as my goal, I can succeed in any amount of time. While I justify postponing a decluttering project until I have time, I can achieve less in fifteen seconds by sticking a too-snug T-shirt straight in the Donate Box.

Less is good.

I Can't Maintain Organized, but I Can Maintain Less

I'd watch those shows where a crew comes in and saves the messy woman from herself. By the time the day-savers wave good-bye, bits and pieces are neatly stored in nooks and crannies, and the home looks wonderful.

I was jealous, but not jealous.

I was jealous of how pretty it all looked. But not jealous because I knew what it was like to have someone come in, put it all away, and leave me with my own personal ta-da. I also knew the satisfaction in the organizer's eyes wouldn't mirror the reality in mine.

Organized friends and relatives have solved my problems many times. I loved it when they were done. The first dozen times, I determined to make it last. I knew what making it last would require. I would have to put things back. Back into the cubby or hole where the organized person had placed it.

But despite all those renewed feelings of determination, I failed. Every time. Eventually, I'd absentmindedly place this or that here or there, and the piles would re-form and the clutter would reappear.

I can maintain less. Instead of worrying about where to put all my stuff, I get rid of things I don't absolutely need and truly use. Sure, I still absentmindedly put things down in the wrong place, but the piles don't form as quickly or grow as tall because there's less. Less stuff forms smaller piles. The stuff that does get scattered is stuff I need and use, so the chances I'll need it again and use it again are 100 percent higher, and each time I use it, the chances are good it will go back in the right place.

And when I do a five-minute pickup as a daily routine, I'm not decluttering. I'm just putting things away—things I use.

Try not getting organized. I think you'll like it.

. . . .

Proof It's Not Just Me

"Moving into a tiny kitchen was really, really hard for my cooking-gadget-obsessed self. Before I bought any 'amazing' space-saving storage organizers, I made myself see what did and didn't fit in cupboards as they were. I got rid of everything whose functions were duplicated, that was broken, or that had never made it out of its packaging. In the end, I only bought one organizer-type thing, *after* I'd learned how my kitchen worked. And now I can breathe, even in my shoebox kitchen. Nothing comes cascading out of the cupboards when I open them and I enjoy it a lot more than I ever liked my giant, overcrowded kitchen!"

—Rachel R.

"The idea of 'just' decluttering has helped me deal with stagnant projects—the ones that you start with so much enthusiasm and then run out of steam (I'm looking at you, deconstructed chairs to be reupholstered!). Rather than finding a better way to store the project and organize all the parts, I can evaluate my time and interest level and maybe . . . 'just' declutter the whole thing from my life."

—Sarah A.

16

Cure Decluttering Paralysis: Do the Easy Stuff First

Fantasy: I need to tackle the most difficult thing first. Once I do that, I can move on and start making progress.

Reality: It's all difficult. Too difficult. I think I'll go take a nap.

Decluttering paralysis is a real thing.

While most people have one space that makes them want to give up before they even start, I had (at least) twenty of those spaces. I had to find a way to cure my own decluttering paralysis.

Do the easy stuff first. Start with trash. Trash is easy.

I feel confident a specific clutter pile is made up completely of last year's school stuff. I'm certain decluttering it will require careful perusal of each item, judgment calls on reusability, and lots of sorting and putting away.

But because my goal is less, I start by looking for trash.

Once I start, I usually find much of the pile is decision-free. Papers wadded up at the bottom of a backpack look like a whole lotta stuff when you don't know what they are, but they're trash. Broken pencils, ripped binders, and used-up paints? Trash.

Once the trash is gone, there's less to deal with. Less is always better.

In my house, a kitchen cabinet usually contains at least a few empty snack boxes or a bag with less than a teaspoon of flour left in it. Those things are trash. Removing them makes a visual impact, and that impact keeps me going.

But after the trash is gone, the heart palpitations start again. There's *still* so much stuff.

When a space is excessively cluttered, it's visually overwhelming. The key to fighting decluttering paralysis is to make the space less visually overwhelming with as little angst as possible.

Do the easy stuff first. Remove things that don't produce moaning or groaning or tears.

At first glance, the teetering pile appears to contain *only* emotionally volatile clutter. Shake your head. Close your eyes. Reopen them and look again.

> Do the easy stuff first. Remove things that don't produce moaning or groaning or tears.

Don't focus on the pile. Focus on one thing. One thing that has a home somewhere other than in that pile. A home established long ago that causes no heart palpitations or decision-making dread whatsoever.

Stop thinking about the big, huge, overwhelming mess, and take that one thing where it goes. Right now.

When you come back to the pile, it will be a little smaller, slightly less overwhelming.

Choose the next easy thing. Take it where it goes. Repeat as long as you keep finding things that are easy.

Every time you move, you're fighting decluttering paralysis. Every time something leaves the pile, you're making progress.

I will use my dining room as an example. (A totally hypothetical example.) When that room has turned into a huge and daunting mess, I have to fight the urge to turn around and pretend it doesn't exist.

Instead, I look for something easy.

The big, green tub full of Christmas decorations sitting in the corner is easy. It doesn't belong in the dining room. It belongs in the garage. There's no angst in that decision because there's no decision to make.

The box is in the dining room because, when we took down our Christmas decorations three months ago, I decided to leave this one box out so I could put away the last of the Christmas towels after they went through the laundry. Leaving that box in the corner of the dining room made complete sense. Now, it's April, and that box has been in the dining room for so long that, at first glance, my brain doesn't register that it is not supposed to be there.

> Every time you move, you're fighting decluttering paralysis. Every time something leaves the pile, you're making progress.

When I remove the box (and take it to the garage immediately), the room is visually less overwhelming because that large, space-taking item is gone.

Now I look for something else that's easy. Something like removing the two or three (or seven) empty Amazon boxes that have been sitting on top of the dining room table for so long I don't even see them anymore.

Then I push in all of the chairs and remove the ones that don't match but have been in there since Christmas dinner. Moving the chairs is easy, but it makes a huge visual impact on the room.

Now, my dining room looks significantly better and I'm less over-whelmed, simply because I did some easy stuff.

Things end up in strange places in our homes. There's usually a good explanation, but it's often forgotten by the time we tackle the space that is now piled up with stuff. I don't have to know how it got there; I just have to take it back where it goes. That's easy.

. . . .

Proof It's Not Just Me

"Doing the easy stuff first has changed the way I look at any project! That initial momentum you need to *just get started* is so hard to overcome. You don't have to do it all in one sitting either—doing the easy stuff first works at all stages. I use this concept at my work as well. Doing the easy stuff first allows me to get started in the morning and just get something done!"

—Lindsay N.

"When I feel overwhelmed because I want it clean *now*, I have to talk myself through it: do the trash first. This gives me momentum! It's cool. Sometimes, I rebel and retort, 'But I don't *know* if *all* of the stuff that looks like trash actually *is* trash!' I tell myself, 'then do the *obvious trash.*' So I grumble my way through, throwing away the obvious trash, and start gaining momentum. Sometimes, before I know it, I've cleaned up and surprised myself."

—Martha R.

"Doing the easy stuff first means something gets done, and something is better than nothing."

—Lucy L.

17

Containers and Limits and How They'll Change Your Life

Fantasy: Containers will make my messy home neat. Someday, I'll find the right containers, and everything I have will be neatly stored, pretty as a magazine, and will stay that way forever.

Reality: My stuff wouldn't fit in the containers I bought, so I bought more containers. It still wouldn't fit. My containers look nothing like the ones in magazines.

When my kids were little bitty, I attended a moms group meeting where an older woman from the church talked about home management. I was skeptical before I went, but I hoped she would be the one to finally give me the lightbulb moment I'd been waiting for.

A lot of things she said made sense, but then she started talking about clutter. She said something about shelf space and asked how much shelf space was worth to us. That we should ask ourselves if this item we were keeping was worth the shelf space.

I was completely lost. I had no clue what she was trying to say. I nodded because everyone else in the room was nodding. They seemed to understand, but I didn't. At all.

And then she casually mentioned the One-In-One-Out Rule. Like it was the most obvious thing ever.

Again, everyone else nodded, and I tried to keep the bewilderment from showing on my face. I felt like she was speaking a different language.

Here's what I understand now that I didn't understand then: it's possible to not have enough room for something in my home.

I used to have a thing for shelves. So many times I found *the* perfect shelf at a garage sale. For only ten bucks (sometimes *five*), *all* of my not-enough-room-for-all-my-junk problems were going to be solved. I'd buy the shelf, and then I'd realize my minivan wasn't big enough to get it home.

I'd call my husband and ask him what to do. He'd heavy-sigh and ask where I thought this shelf was going to go. I'd roll my eyes like that was *such* a dumb question. I mean, it was a *shelf*. A shelf *solves* clutter problems; it can't *be* clutter!

> Here's what I understand now that I didn't understand then: it's possible to not have enough room for something in my home.

After we figured out how to get it home, I dragged my beautiful new shelf through the garage into my cluttered house. I looked around and realized I *didn't* actually know where I was going to put it.

Oh well, it could wait in the garage until I figured something out. Someday, when I get organized, I'll be so glad I already have this shelf. The shelf that was only ten bucks! How smart I'll feel when I won't have to run out and buy one for ten times that much, like all those other not-as-smart-as-me suckers would!

But then one day, as I tried to organize my kitchen, I realized what the speaker had been saying and why my overabundance of shelves hadn't made my house any more organized.

As I worked, I decided to designate a cookbook shelf in the pantry. My cookbooks had been piled precariously on top of my refrigerator for years.

I had enough cookbooks to fill a shelf and a half, but I only had one shelf to give.

My natural, slob-logical solution? Add another shelf. Buy more furniture for my already full kitchen until we had enough money to buy a new house. A bigger house with room for all my cookbooks.

But those tendencies were what got me into this desperate-enough-to-start-an-anonymous-slob-blog state, so I tried to think of another way.

I suddenly realized what organizers meant when they casually mentioned an item deserving shelf space. *The shelf was a limit.*

The size of the shelf determined how many cookbooks I could keep. I didn't need to figure out where to put the ones that didn't fit on the shelf. I didn't need to lay the extras across the top of other books (like I had always done before). Instead, I needed to decide which cookbooks deserved to be on the shelf, and get rid of the ones that didn't fit.

This was my lightbulb moment.

I started viewing my cookbooks according to shelf-worthiness. I filled the shelf with my favorite ones first. Once the shelf was full, I knew the leftover cookbooks were the ones I didn't like as much. They weren't shelf-worthy.

The shelf was an impersonal limit. Once I acknowledged that limit, I didn't have to agonize over how many cookbooks to keep. The size of the shelf made that decision for me.

I'd never considered that I had most- or least-favorite cookbooks. I liked cookbooks in general. I liked what they represented and the possibilities they contained. But once I realized the size of the shelf determined how many I could keep, I saw clearly which ones I liked best. My angst was gone.

But alas, my happy ending was threatened within the hour. Once I squeezed in all the cookbooks I could squeeze and placed the less-shelf-worthy ones in the Donate Box, the inevitable happened.

I found . . . one more. I found one more cookbook I really liked. I maybe even loved it.

Because I had no faith in my own organizing abilities, I was scared. Things like this *always* happen. I think I've solved a problem, and then something, usually sooner than later, ruins everything.

But then, suddenly, I understood the One-In-One-Out Rule.

The One-In-One-Out Rule is a principle used by every organizer anywhere. That speaker at the moms group stated it (just the name of it, not an explanation of it) as a quick and easy answer to one of the questions someone asked. I pretended I had a clue, but I didn't.

In case you don't, here's what the One-In-One-Out Rule means. Once you understand that keeping everything isn't possible in any home ever (that wants to not be crazypants) and you understand the space you have available is a natural limit, *then* you understand that when something new comes in, something old has to leave to make room.

Real room. *Not* shove-it-in-anyway room.

As a shover, I didn't get this. If the drawer didn't close, I blamed the drawer and thought I needed more drawers. It never occurred to me I had too many things in the drawer because I didn't know the drawer was a natural limit.

Swapping one for one wouldn't make any difference whatsoever. If I got new socks and swapped out the new pair for an old pair, the drawer still wouldn't close. What difference would that make, so why bother?

Duh. I had too many socks.

I honestly didn't know it was possible to have too many socks. Socks are really good things to have! The One-In-One-Out Rule didn't make sense because limits didn't make sense.

But once I realized the shelf determined how many cookbooks I could keep, I realized that in order to justify keeping the recently found cookbook, I had to decide which book on the shelf I liked the least. Remove that one; replace it with the one I loved.

Angst? None. The shelf made the hard decision for me. I didn't have to decide how many cookbooks a woman of my kitchen prowess really needs. All I had to do was choose which cookbook I liked the least.

Soon after this space-in-my-home-doesn't-expand-to-fit-all-the-stuff-I-want realization, I grasped that the root word of *container* is *contain*.

Like that shelf, containers are limits. When firefighters fight a wildfire, they focus on containing it. A wildfire is a fire that gets out of control. It spreads.

My house was out of control.

If I focused on one small area, another burst into clutter. While I shifted my brainpower to that new area, the clutter crept back into the first one.

Containers contain. They limit. They hold the stuff in and keep it from spreading.

When a container is full, I know how much I can keep. If I try to shove more into the container than will fit (like I used to do), the stuff spills out and turns into clutter.

Fire contained in a fire pit is good. Fire growing so big it moves outside the fire pit is bad. Very bad and very scary.

Stuff that turns into clutter grows. That's scary too.

Decluttering was difficult because my clutter was personal. I possessed each thing for some good reason. It had been on sale. Someone had given it to me. I'd had a great idea, bought the supplies, and was waiting until I could act on that idea.

> If I focused on one small area, another burst into clutter. While I shifted my brainpower to that new area, the clutter crept back into the first one.

I stressed and fretted. I imagined scenarios in which I'd use each random thing and wished for places to store it all.

Grasping the Container Concept changed how I viewed my home.

The Container Concept eliminated (or significantly lessened) the pressure to decide whether I loved or hated something enough to keep it or purge it. As an anthropomorphist who, as a child, avoided kissing one of her dolls because then she'd have to spend an hour kissing the other fifty (so as not to show favoritism), this was agonizing.

Once I understood containers, I realized the decision wasn't up to me. The container made the decision. I don't have to answer "Will I ever need this?" I just have to determine if it fits. Whether it fits isn't personal—it's fact.

For example, craft supplies. I love pretty pictures of bins and baskets filled with neatly sorted markers and crayons and paper scraps.

My craft cabinet didn't look like that. Mine was a jumbled mess, and when I tried to clean it up and sort it out, I became frustrated.

I didn't understand the containers in those pretty pictures were actually containing. They were limiting.

If I had more beads than would fit into a container, I thought I needed another container. When the second container was full, I bought a third and then a fourth. If the fourth wouldn't fit onto the shelf, I started filling the next shelf with these containers full of beads. Then I had no room for paints or paper or scissors.

Once I understood containers were limits, I realized I couldn't keep all the beads. I could only keep the ones that fit in the container. This awakened me from my slob coma, and I realized I could survive with one container of beads. Only one. (Or maybe two.)

Understanding the Container Concept showed me it was okay to get rid of perfectly good beads. I didn't *have to* keep them because they were perfectly good. I *couldn't* keep them because I didn't have the room. The container made that decision for me.

> The solution to my clutter problem is not to find another container, add a new shelving unit, build a new room, or buy a new home. The solution to my clutter problem is letting my house be my container.

I started to see how the Container Concept applies on every level. The container determined the number of beads I could keep. The shelf determined how many containers I could have. The size of the room determined how many shelves I could have.

The solution for my clutter problem is not to find another container, add a new shelving unit, build a new room, or buy a new home. The solution to my clutter problem is letting my house be my container. I can't fit more into it than will fit in the space it provides.

The size of my drawers and closets determines how many clothes I can have. The size of my bedroom determines how many drawers and closets I can have. My house determines what is a bedroom, and I'm not willing to sacrifice my kitchen to have more space for clothes.

The Container Concept will change your life.

. . . .

Proof It's Not Just Me

"I always figured if I ran out of room for items, I needed more storage space (bins, baskets, shelves, etc.). The Container Concept has changed my life! I now see every area of my home as a "container." Kitchen drawers and cabinets, my closets, my dresser drawers, even whole rooms and our deck! If something doesn't fit in the ready-made 'container,' it's time to purge! The Container Concept also helps me avoid impulse buys when I ask myself, 'What container will this item go into? Is there room for it right now?'"

—Melinda P.

"The Container Concept has changed the way I shop. I would buy things without giving pause to think about how those items worked in the space I had. This equaled clutter city. Now, when I buy something, I know where it will go and what it will add to my home. This also encourages me to part with things that aren't 'pulling their weight' in the container. If all my socks have to fit in one drawer, I'm not going to keep that single Santa sock with holes in it that I have had for fifteen years."

—Emily N.

"After this epiphany on container-ing, we ended up redoing my daughter's room. There are clear bins with *lids*. If the lid doesn't close, she has a choice to make. Mommy doesn't have to be the bad guy. For stuffies, she has a cabinet. The doors must shut. She *hates* the entire concept for her stuffies, but magically, she has stopped asking for more and has stopped spending her money on them. *Victorious!*"

—Celina B.

"When my father-in-law recently told me about a tremendous sale on a cute little set of teacups on eBay, I knew I had made a breakthrough when my thinking process went like this: 'Oh, they are nice—and a great deal. But my teacup storage space is already full of teacups. I would have to make more space for these or break the ones I have in order to justify buying more.' Even though my first thought was of destruction . . . it's certainly a step in the right direction!"

—Jerica C.

"We have nine people in our household and *tons* of blankets. I have a huge Rubbermaid bin that is supposed to house them. It usually works because the kids have 8–10 of them out of the bin at any given time. Well, I decided to clean and organize, and those blankets did *not* fit in the container anymore. So, I sorted them. I kept the really nice, warm ones. Baby blankets that were handmade got packed away for my eventual grandchildren. Other nonsentimental blankets (usually the cheap fleece ones) were donated. The blankets left are the ones we actually like, and they always fit back in the bin. Such freedom!"

—Sheri B.

18

....

Find Your Clutter Threshold

Fantasy: I need this stuff. I mean, not right now, but someday I'll be glad I already have it.
Reality: I can't handle this stuff. The house is a wreck, and I can't find the things I need when I need them.

You have a Clutter Threshold. We each have one.

How is my neighbor's seashell display so artsy-fartsy, but mine looks like a crab family died on my bookshelf? How does her art supply cabinet look like art, but mine is a pile of scribbled-on papers, broken crayons, and dried-up paintbrushes?

My Clutter Threshold is different from hers. We can own the exact same items, but hers stay under control, while mine morph into a pile of clutter.

Every person has a Clutter Threshold that determines what constitutes clutter in each unique home. I'm not talking about clutter tolerance (or Slob Vision: my amazing ability to not see piles of stuff until they're completely out of control). My Clutter Threshold is the point at which I have more stuff than I can keep under control—the point at which my stuff turns into clutter.

Have you ever walked into someone's home who has the same tastes as you? You see she likes quilts and old movies. You admire a color-coordinated display of her grandmother's quilts and strike up a conversation as you shift your head to the right and read the titles of her favorite films.

Then you go home.

Shoving *your* grandma's quilt to the other end of the couch so you have a place to sit, you notice your own DVDs piled whompyjawed on the floor next to the TV. You stare into space, wishing you understood why your house doesn't look like hers.

Three Homes I Liked but Couldn't Create

In college, I spent a weekend at a friend's house. Her family liked the same kinds of cool stuff I liked. They were the definition of eclectic. Having been the kid who dreamed of owning a junkyard, their style was the look I wanted to achieve in my future home.

I remember shelves full of interesting things, all artfully displayed. Antique toys, scientific instruments, handwritten notes on yellowed paper framed and arranged just so. They even had a doll room. I wasn't into dolls, but I made a mental note to make a Room of Something. Something cool.

I could gaze for hours at the stuff in any room in that home. It was like staying in a museum or at least one of those funky restaurants with memorabilia everywhere.

But even though I was awesome at collecting stuff, I wasn't awesome at displaying it. This didn't bother me until I moved into my first real home. (Dorm rooms and college apartments, and even our first rental when we got married, didn't count.)

I'd arrange some of my favorite things on a shelf, but within a week, the favorite things started blending in with clutter.

But I kept collecting. I liked having options. My options sat in bags and boxes and piles, but I was sure that when I finally figured out how I wanted to decorate I'd be glad to have so much cool stuff from which to choose.

Then, the second house.

In the midst of my most frustrating of frustrating times over the state of my home, I visited a friend. I complimented her new wall hangings. She launched into a story about how much she had stressed over what to put on her walls. She looked and looked and finally decided to buy these.

They looked great. Her home looked great. It was lovely and inviting. And even though it wasn't my own undefinable style, I was jealous. She had something on her wall and didn't have closets full of things that *might* one day go on her wall.

I had closets and rooms and a garage full of possibilities—and nothing on my walls.

I wanted the design of that first house. I collected like that family had collected, but I couldn't achieve the look they achieved.

I admired the second house. It looked nice, felt comfortable, and was completely under control. But the concept of not having options was completely foreign to me.

And then there's the third house we need to discuss: my mother's house. My mother, the most influential person in my life.

Before I start psychoanalyzing her home, let me clarify that she has been nothing but supportive on this deslobification journey and the broadcast of it to the world. She is very understanding when I talk about her publicly.

In fact, she is the reason I knew (though I hated to admit it to myself) that a professional organizer would not solve my Slob Problems. She was my professional organizer, at my beck and call every time I needed her. She'd come in, clean up, implement genius "systems," and I would swear to myself I was going to keep it that way.

Every time she leaves a room, it's neater than it was when she got there.

But she likes to be prepared. For *any* possibility. For any end-of-the-world event that could happen. Some might term it an obsession.

If you need to outfit fifty kids in traditional dress from fifty countries, ask my mom. She knows exactly where she keeps her kid-sized international costumes. If you need to decorate for a wedding that's happening next weekend, she'll set you up. If you need to feed a family of ten for a month after every grocery store in the country has gone out of business, go to her house.

She's not overly sentimental, but she's excessively practical.

This was normal to me. I inherited her mind-set, but I didn't inherit her ability to keep it under control. I didn't understand that for a long time.

I liked my mind-set. When my church needed cowboy boots to decorate for an event, I'm sure they expected various people to lend a pair or two each. I proudly walked in carrying a forty-gallon storage tub full of boots in all sizes and asked if someone could help me carry in the other two tubs.

I saved the day, y'all. Not that anything bad would have happened if we hadn't had enough cowboy boots, but I got a thrill from the admiration and wonder (and concern?) on people's faces as they struggled to understand why anyone would have so many pairs of cowboy boots.

I had a totally logical reason. Cowboy boots sold on eBay. I bought them at Texas garage sales for a dollar or less and sold them the next fall for way more than a dollar. The obvious-to-everyone-else downside of needing to store large numbers of things I didn't personally use was a nonissue in my brain. I never even thought about that as a problem.

Finding My Clutter Threshold

As I *just* decluttered and lived in a home with less, I noticed my house stayed under control for longer periods of time—and with less effort.

A big part of my slob problem all along was that I was living above my Clutter Threshold, because I didn't know about such a thing. I had inherited my mother's mind-set, but I did not inherit her ability to keep the stuff required for that mind-set under control. I didn't inherit her Clutter Threshold. Mine is much lower than my mother's. I can't handle the amount of stuff she can handle. She sorts into boxes and bins and packs it all away neatly. I shove things here and there and can never find what I need when I need it.

> Anything I can't handle, that continually gets out of control, is clutter.

Anything I can't handle, that continually gets out of control, is clutter. My mother and the Eclectic Family have high Clutter Thresholds. They can handle a lot of stuff and keep it all under control so the stuff doesn't turn into clutter. Stuff comes into their homes, and they know where to put it. My friend with the wall hangings has a low Clutter Threshold, but she knows her threshold is low (without knowing or caring what a Clutter Threshold is). She doesn't bring stuff into her house without knowing she has a place for it.

I have a low Clutter Threshold, but I didn't know it. I kept bringing stuff into my house and was surprised when it kept turning into clutter.

The Thing About a Place for Everything

If you're anything like me, someone cheerily (and totally judgmentally) chanting "A place for everything and everything in its place" sounds like fingernails on a chalkboard. It's maddening. And irritating. And not the least bit helpful when someone tries to solve your problems with one cute little saying.

I understand what the phrase means. Now I get how the concept works, and I know what wasn't working in my home.

If you have too much stuff (like I did), there isn't a place for everything. There just isn't. Don't start by looking for a place for everything.

I tried to shove all my stuff into random places, pushing and grunting to make it all fit.

I admired the results of my efforts for a few seconds until I needed something I'd just shoved somewhere. While I searched, the house morphed right back into its previous state of disaster.

A place for everything will happen, but it will happen gradually, eventually, as you declutter. Focus on getting stuff you don't need out of your house. Use your understanding of the true definition of clutter (anything you can't easily keep under control) and ask yourself, "Can I handle this?" instead of "Should I keep this?"

As you experience less and as you follow the strategies I'm giving you to tackle your clutter, you'll slowly find a place for everything. It will still be an annoying phrase, but you'll get the beauty of the concept.

Stop Stuff Shifting

Are you a stuff shifter? I was. Big time.

When I hosted anything at my home, the first step of my two-week preparation was decluttering.

Actually, I *thought* I was decluttering, but I was really just shifting my stuff. I was taking the top layer (things with no real "place") to the master bedroom. That room locks, so guests couldn't stumble upon my clutter secret.

The problem happened when the party was over. While I was loving my home and wondering why in the world I couldn't keep it this way, I had two choices.

I could continue using the master bedroom as a storage space, or I could reclutter the rooms I cleaned for the party. Usually, I wouldn't choose and eventually got a mix of both. The master bedroom stayed full of junk, while bits and pieces drifted out and re-cluttered the rest of the house.

If you're a stuff shifter, you're living above your Clutter Threshold. The only solution is less.

Once Everything Has a Place

Less is a beautiful thing. Less stuff means less tripping, less bumping, and fewer clutter avalanches. Less means Disaster Status is less overwhelming, less time-consuming to recover from, and more easily fixed.

For people like me, Disaster Status is going to happen. Happening less often and being less disastrous is a huge improvement.

Experiencing easier recovery from Disaster Status is how I finally grasped the beauty of there being a place for everything.

Having a place for everything is how Normal People clean up their homes so easily. It's how they avoid standing in the middle of a messy room, holding a plastic harmonica and fighting back tears.

Once you've decluttered to the point where you have only what you can handle, disaster recovery is about putting things away. *That's it.*

It's not about deciding what to do with all your stuff. Putting things away is just a matter of moving them from one spot to another, no angst-ridden decision-making involved.

Having a place for everything doesn't mean everything is always in its place; it simply means everything has a place to go.

This Is How Normal People Do It

Was that the first time I have referred to Normal People? Oh. I hope you aren't offended. I call nonslobs Normal People. It's a term of endearment. Just know no one is actually normal, and normal is usually the opposite of fun and exciting.

I want to be sure I share what I've observed about how Normal People keep their homes uncluttered. They err on the side of getting rid of things. Normal People naturally ask why they should keep something instead of the rhetorical "Why not?" question that slobs favor. Basically, they're born knowing their Clutter Threshold, and they live within it.

The Thing About Storage Space

A favorite excuse for people like me is a lack of storage space. For years, I embraced my lack of closets and storage buildings and attics that don't turn into ovens in Texas's August heat as the reason my home was a disaster.

I finally realized my house was a container, but even though that understanding helped me limit what I could keep, I still begrudged the fact that we didn't have nooks and crannies available for storing the things I truly needed to keep, like gift wrap and out-of-season clothing and such. These things inhabited corners of my master bedroom or our game room and blended into the cluttered scenery. The things were continually shifted from place to place, until I learned to apply the One-In-One-Out Rule on a much larger scale.

When I find myself Stuff Shifting entire groups of homeless items, I now know to look for storage space in my own home. If we really need this stuff, it needs a designated space. Floating from the master bedroom to the kitchen isn't an option in a livable home.

To clear my Slob Vision, I shake my head and walk around my house. If I see a cabinet I know is full, but I can't remember exactly what is inside, there's a decent chance I haven't used whatever is inside in a very long time. I open the cabinet. If I find a mishmash of random things, I can usually declutter that space to make room for things I know I need. (Don't worry, exact decluttering steps are coming up soon.)

> If I truly need and use something on a regular basis, that thing deserves space in my home more than random things I almost never use.

If I truly need and use something on a regular basis, that thing deserves space in my home more than random things I almost never use.

This concept can apply to entire rooms and has an even more beautiful effect. For the first three years we lived in this house, our game room was my eBay room. My heart still feels heavy when I remember the state of that room. Other than a path between the room's two main doors, the floor was covered with boxes and piles. A six-foot-long double hanging rack filled with clothing took up the back third of the room.

Once I began purging in earnest and stopped the inflow of things to sell, something strange happened. My house grew. Literally, but not literally. My home gained more than four hundred square feet.

Four hundred *usable* square feet.

Want to know the best part? We also gained a half-bath. I had an extra *bathroom* in the back corner of that room. We never used it because we couldn't get to it, so I mostly forgot that bathroom existed.

Once the room was no longer a container for things I didn't even use, the room contained us. Now, the game room is my favorite feature of this house. My boys spend Friday nights playing video games in there. My daughter sets up classes for her stuffed animals. If one child's friend spends the night, they have a space to hang out, away from annoying siblings. And, very best of all, I have an easy-to-clean half-bath to which I can send our guests.

If you struggle to keep stuff from overtaking your home, I can guess you've dreamed of having a bigger house. I did. Literally. One of my recurring dreams was that I found rooms in my home that I didn't know existed.

That dream came true when I decluttered our game room and we started living in it. We removed the things we didn't need, and the things we do need, like books and jackets and craft supplies, now have a home.

Proof It's Not Just Me

"I realized my thinking had subtly shifted when faced with a sale on my favorite toothpaste. I remembered I still had one or two tubes at home and decided I would rather take a chance that I would have to buy the toothpaste later at a higher price than find a place to store the discounted toothpaste. Baby steps, I know, but having that moment gave me hope that I was beginning to understand the limits of my Slob Brain."

—Meghan H.

"If something has a place, it's easy to take it there when you find it lying around the house. Things that don't have a place get shuffled around, causing clutter."

—Brandi D.

19

How to Prioritize Decluttering Projects: The Visibility Rule

Fantasy: I'm going to change my slobbish ways and get rid of my clutter. All of it. This closet is full from top to bottom with stuff I probably don't need. I'll start here so I can make big progress today.

Reality: I spend all day working on a closet I never open, and I have nothing to show for all my work because I never open the closet. My house doesn't look any better when I'm done.

The physical urge to declutter is a very real thing. Sometimes I feel like my skin is crawling, I'm just so tired of the stuff. Sometimes tears threaten to spill (or pour) down my face when I've lost my keys—again. Sometimes it seems like there's a sandbag sitting on my chest and I'm drowning in a sea of stuff.

This happens to everyone. I've heard it even happens to Normal People.

Every time I had one of those bursts of decluttering energy, acted on it, wore myself out, and then found that my house didn't look a bit different when I was done, I grew more and more cynical about ever making any real progress. The next time I experienced a burst of decluttering energy, my cynicism talked me into eating ice cream instead.

This hopeless cycle ended when I created the Visibility Rule.

People like me get the urge to declutter and head straight for a storage closet as a starting place. My storage closet is obviously cluttered, and if I declutter it, the closet might actually *stay* decluttered, since we rarely open it.

Using my decluttering energy on a space that will stay decluttered makes sense. Isn't that how I'll make progress?

I think I've established that things rarely work out the way my slob logic predicts they will.

Here's what really happens: I work on the storage closet. It's a big job. It's full of stuff I shoved in there because I didn't have a place for it in the house. I didn't have a place for it in the house because I wasn't totally sure I needed it.

The storage closet is full of decisions. Decisions stress me out, and stress makes me tired. By the time I'm done, I'm *done*. My decluttering energy is spent.

> Things rarely work out the way my slob logic predicts they will.

I close the closet door, but when I turn around, my house doesn't look any better than it did before I started. All the work I did is hidden behind a door.

The next day, I never think about decluttering. I forget my decision to declutter the entire house, and there's nothing visible to remind me. My Slob Vision returns, and I go on with life in my cluttered home.

Our daily life doesn't benefit. Maybe I'll smile when I open the storage closet on a random Tuesday, but I don't gain momentum or energy to keep decluttering.

Follow the Visibility Rule

The Visibility Rule: When I feel the urge to declutter, I start with visible clutter.

I stop. I look around. I let my brain register which out-in-the-open space is piled with stuff.

I have to consciously (and often verbally) remind myself to follow the Visibility Rule, because if I don't, these out-in-the-open cluttered spaces are invisible to me. My everyday brain doesn't see them because it has grown accustomed to the clutter.

I stand at my front door and look at my home as a visitor would see it. Suddenly, I see the pile of mail on top of the piano.

I hate that stupid pile of mail, but it passes the Visibility Test. It's visible clutter. It makes my house look messy. If I ignore it, my house will still look messy even if I clean all day.

The pile of mail is visible, so it needs to be tackled first. That's the deciding, prioritizing factor.

Sometimes visible clutter isn't as dramatic as a pile of papers. Sometimes it's almost-empty chip bags or an only-the-heels-left bread bag on the kitchen counter. Sometimes it's a "temporary" pile of laundry on the recliner in the living room.

If you're a Normal Person, and you're reading this, I know what you're thinking: *That's not a decluttering project; that's just housework. That's cleaning up and putting things away.*

You're right, of course. But this book isn't for you, so I'll explain for the people whose brains work like mine: people like me view stuff like that as a project, and projects are put-offable, so we put them off.

When I follow the Visibility Rule, a crazy thing happens. Once I've decluttered (or just plain cleared off) the dining room table, the dining room table is clear.

Even though my Slob Vision prevented me from noticing the piles of stuff, I *do* notice when it's clear. Every time I walk by the table, my heart does a happy little flip. My face lights up with a smile. I'm encouraged to keep going. The results of this visible decluttering project increase my decluttering energy.

And . . . my family has dinner at our clean table, and I feel more warm fuzzies. This decluttering project improved how my family functions and improved our daily lives.

The next day, I notice again how nice my dining table looks, and I do a little more decluttering in another visible place. *That* visible progress inspires me to do more, and suddenly I have traction.

If you prioritize decluttering projects by visibility, you'll see real changes in your home.

. . . .

Proof It's Not Just Me

"When I first read about the Visibility Rule, it felt like permission to take a deep breath and stop feeling paralyzed by how disorganized my stuff is. The more often the 'surface' is clean, the more often I feel ready to tackle those spots. I feel a lot happier with my home, even if it isn't that much more organized. It's a lot nicer to look at anyway!"

—Rachel R.

"I love to tidy a hidden space, a junk drawer or cupboard. You know, something that doesn't affect my everyday life! The Visibility Rule helps me to focus on something useful, which will inspire me to keep working."

—Jacqui K.

20

Two (and Only Two) Decluttering Questions

Fantasy: If I make myself answer some really hard questions, I'll figure out which of my things are worthy of staying.

Reality: I have too much stuff. A lot of it is trash.

You're tackling visible spaces. You're doing the easy stuff first. You're identifying (and going against) your natural inclinations that kept you from making progress in the past. You might even feel like you're gaining coveted and oft-elusive traction.

But you will always come across an item (or twenty) that makes you stop and stammer. You hold it in your hand, staring into space, for way too long.

I came across many of these things. I would often say one of my biggest frustrations with decluttering was that I never knew what to do when I got down to the little stuff. Stuff I legitimately might need one day but that I had no idea where to put.

I've seen lists. I've read books and blog posts and magazine articles and heard interviews where organizing experts give eight or ten (or sometimes more) questions to ask yourself when you need to decide if you should get rid of something.

Grandma's step stool? That probably deserves a ten-question list.

A pack of glow-in-the-dark bracelets? It doesn't deserve that kind of energy. There was a time, though, when small and inconsequential things produced total decluttering panic in my heart.

I had too much stuff. More stuff than people who make up ten-question lists could ever imagine. I simply could not devote the time and energy to asking myself ten questions about each item.

I also couldn't afford to base any of my decluttering decisions on emotions, and so many of the typical decluttering questions deal in emotions. I have an overactive imagination, and my creative brain breeds ideas like rabbits. Do those glow in the dark bracelets make me happy? Well, now that I think about it, they really do. They remind me of a time in my life when my oldest child was in kindergarten. They're the leftovers the teacher sent home after his kindergarten class took a "trip to the moon." Each child received a box full of trinkets, and the teacher assigned glow-in-the-dark bracelets to me to bring for all of the kids. My little boy was so innocent then. So sweet. I remember his excitement when school was new and every day was wonderful. In his six-year-old mind, he really *was* taking a trip to the moon! That was such a good year. I miss the simplicity of kindergarten. Of reading a list of three-letter words for homework. Of all the kids getting along and liking one another and feeling excitement over glow-in-the-dark bracelets.

Well, that little daydream wasted *way* too much of my precious decluttering time.

As I picked up ridiculous numbers of things Normal People would never have kept in the first place, I came up with two simple questions to ask myself. These two questions work every time. And if I can answer the first one, I don't even have to *ask* the second one.

Decluttering Question #1: If I Were Looking for This Item, Where Would I Look for It First?

This is not an analytical question. I love analytical questions way too much. I can analyze all day long. But one little word keeps me from going down the analyzation path.

Would.

Not *should.*

Would instead of *should* is the key. *Would* depends on instinct. It's a first reaction. *Should* depends on reasoning. Reasoning can go on all day.

Instead of asking myself where *should* I look for something, I ask where *would* I look for it.

Just to be clear, I'm not asking where I would *put* something. I'm asking where I would *look* for it. "Where would I look?" is an easier question. I can hem and haw all day about where to put something. But if I needed it and went looking, it's pretty easy to say where I'd go first in my search.

Simplifying my home starts with simplifying the questions I ask myself. Overthinking is a big part of my problem.

Asking *would* instead of *should* means I have to accept that my instinct, my very first thought, is okay.

When I overthink, I try to come up with the best place to put something. The place where it will be at home for the next twenty years. Trying to predict the next twenty years is a lot of pressure. So many variables. We could remodel the house! Or move! Who knows what life will hold and how that will affect where I should put this box of safety pins?

None of that matters. The only thing that matters is where I'd look first if I needed a safety pin *today*. The place where I'd look first is the place where it needs to go.

Even if it feels *wrong*. Or second best. Or opposite of where I'm sure an organized person would put it in her house. Surely, she'd keep safety pins in her sewing box. She'd know exactly where that box was and would go straight to it in any safety-pin emergency.

I don't use safety pins often. I have a sewing box (and two sewing machines), but I don't sew. As someone who doesn't actually sew, I don't automatically look for my "sewing box" in the moment when I need to pin up the hem of the dress I need to wear.

I look in my junk drawer. That's the first place I look when I need a safety pin, so that's where safety pins go. It doesn't matter how much more logical and practical other places seem when I stop to think about where safety pins *should* go.

Don't stop. Don't think. Just answer the question. Where would I look for it?

In the junk drawer? Then that's where it goes.

Going with this instinct prevents stress now and prevents stress later. Where I'd look for it first is an angst-free answer—and when I do look for it, I'll find it in the first place I look! That's a miracle in my home!

There's a second part of this question; it isn't a question, but it's very important.

"Take it there right now."

Once you've answered "Where would I look for it?" with your first instinct, take it to that place now. Right now. I'll go into excruciating detail explaining why in the next chapter, but for now I'll tell you this is the one thing that will help you make progress no matter when you get distracted from this particular decluttering project.

Once you take it there, you're done. Move on to the next item.

But if you ask question number one and your answer is "Hamana hamana, um, wellll . . . ," move on to question number two.

Decluttering Question #2: If I Needed This Item, Would It Ever Occur to Me That I Already Had One?

This question is hard. I'm looking at this thing. Right this very second, I know I have it *because it's in my hand.* But was it a surprise when I found it?

If I didn't know I had it, I would never look for it. If I never even looked for it, I'd go out and buy another one. Then I'd have two.

I don't need to add more stuff to what I already have.

If the answer to question number two is "no," I need to stick it in the Donate Box. There is no point in keeping something I didn't even know I had.

I couldn't answer the first decluttering question because I *wouldn't* look. The thought wouldn't even *occur* to me to look for it.

I'm not saying this isn't hard. It's very hard. Sometimes, decluttering feels like Christmas. I generally have no idea what I'm going to find. I see this item, remember why I brought it home, reimagine the scenario when I kept it the first time, and try to convince myself maybe *now* I'll finally use it.

I can't go there. I couldn't answer Decluttering Question #1 because there wasn't an answer. I wouldn't have looked for it because I had no idea I had one.

My debilitating frugality complicates the issue even more. The thought of paying *again* for something I once decluttered feels ridiculously wasteful. Painfully wasteful. But what's more wasteful? Spending three dollars to buy more glow-in-the-dark bracelets? Or paying a mortgage on a house where we can't live comfortably because it's so full of stuff and *then* paying three dollars for glow-in-the-dark bracelets when I already have some, but don't even *know* I have them because they're buried under a pile of stuff?

> But what's more wasteful? Spending three dollars to buy more glow-in-the-dark bracelets? Or paying a mortgage on a house where we can't live comfortably because it's so full of stuff?

The second one. The second one is more wasteful.

Oh, you'll regret getting rid of those bracelets. I'm not pretending you won't. When you need them, you'll remember you had them, even though you didn't know you had them when you actually had them.

How do you deal with this regret? Get over it. Feel the pain, and move on with your life.

Sorry.

Those glow-in-the-dark bracelets cost three dollars. If I need them six weeks later, it is worth three dollars to have lived in my decluttered home for those six weeks.

Proof It's Not Just Me

"I have been using the two decluttering questions for about two months now. 'Where would I look for this first?' helps me put things where my husband and I can both find them. So many times he'll look for something in what I think is a crazy place, but if I move that thing there, he doesn't have to ask me where everything is anymore."

—Melissa H.

21

How to Declutter Without Making a Bigger Mess

Fantasy: A clean slate is the best way to create the perfect room. I'll just pull out everything and then only put back the things I need.

Reality: Distractions are the one guarantee in my life. The chances of me completely finishing every last bit of this decluttering project are slim to none. When I have to stop, the stuff I pulled out of this cluttered space will be all over the floor, outside of the area where, before, it was at least hidden.

Every time I try to declutter, I end up making a bigger mess!"
This is the biggest complaint declutterers have. It's not just you, I promise.

It was my own complaint too. I'd get the decluttering bug and start pulling everything out of the space I was tackling. Pulling everything out makes perfect sense in a perfect world. If nothing ever happened to distract me and I could guarantee I'd finish this project before I needed to move on to things like eating or sleeping or bandaging wounds, I'd be fine.

Is it possible to declutter without making a bigger mess?

Yes. I can tell you how in one little sentence you read in the last chapter. "Take it there right now."

Remember that sentence? It's the second part of the first decluttering question. It's the part that has the biggest impact on your decluttering progress, even though it does not fit in with my elaborate fantasies of extreme efficiency.

Did you read *Cheaper by the Dozen* as a kid? I loved that book. The stories of the big family were hilarious, but my soul was energized by the father's obsession with efficiency. Like when he had the tonsils of *all* his children removed, *in his own house*, and studied the process for the purpose of making tonsillectomies more efficient.

I would totally do that. If I had twelve kids and could talk a doctor into doing it in my house (so it wouldn't break us financially) and had anyone in the universe who would care what I had to say about the efficiency of tonsillectomies.

I really wouldn't. But I eat those kinds of stories up.

I lo-o-ove the cartoons where the cat (or mouse or whatever other anthropomorphic character) uses a complicated, twenty-seven-step machine to toast a piece of bread. Those contraptions are awesome and so well thought out! Sure, they require months of planning and weeks of implementation to do a task that could be done by simply removing bread from the bag and walking over to the toaster and pushing the button, but, y'all, the cat *didn't even have to get out of bed* once it was done!

My effiency-obsessed-to-the-point-of-making-things-harder-than-they-should-be brain wants to declutter like this:

1. Pull everything out of the space.
2. Once it's all out, sort it into piles according to where things will go in the house.
3. Put back the things I want in that space.
4. Walk (dramatically) through the house, delivering items to their proper homes.

I've decluttered this way. I totally get why it works for other people. It just doesn't work for me.

Everything goes great until I get to step 2 or some random point within that task. This random point might occur when a child enters the room sobbing because our puppy just chewed up her library book. It might happen when I realize it's time to pick up my son from football practice. I might leave the project area to use the restroom, walk through the kitchen, and remember I need to put dinner in the slow cooker, completely forgetting I was in the middle of a decluttering project.

The sorting is the problem. Sorting in this way leaves room for "later." I have to get rid of any opportunities for later when I declutter. My attention span and my available time and my caring-whatsoever-about-this-mess are not guaranteed to exist in Later Land, so I can't go there.

> My attention span and my available time and my caring-whatsoever-about-this-mess are not guaranteed to exist in Later Land, so I can't go there.

Decluttering that creates a bigger mess is decluttering that depends on later.

Here's how "take it there right now" plays out.

I start a decluttering project with the correct supplies:

1. A black trash bag
2. A donatable Donate Box
3. My feet

The Black Trash Bag

The black trash bag is for . . . trash. The trash bag doesn't have to be black, but black is ideal in case I'm throwing away something the mini-people in my home might suddenly remember is their long-lost favorite thing in the whole wide world. There's always trash: bottle caps and broken pens and fast-food receipts.

If you have an established and accessible recycling routine, grab that container as well. If you don't, and this bothers you greatly, reread chapter 3 and remember your goal is to reduce the amount of stuff in your home and the amount of overwhelm you feel so that, one day, you *can* handle being as green as you want to be.

Trash is easy. Bringing the trash bag to the site of the project makes it easy to pitch.

The Donatable Donate Box

The key word (that isn't actually a word) here is *donatable*. No pretty tubs or baskets with the word *donations* stenciled on the side. If the box is pretty, you'll want to keep it for the next decluttering project. We're not keeping this Donate Box. The box is going to be donated too.

You know how decluttering can feel like it never ends? You know how those feelings and frustrations can keep you from starting in the first place? And how not starting in the first place is the reason your home gets more and more cluttered and makes you feel like you're drowning? Our goal is to eliminate the "never-ending-project" feeling.

Once you answer Decluttering Question #2 (If I needed this, would it ever occur to me that I already had it?) with a no, you're done. You are finished with that item forever. It's in the Donate Box, and you never have to touch it or think about it or make that decision again.

A Donate Box that has to be emptied before its contents can be donated is a recipe for disaster for people like me. Those kinds of Donate Boxes are boxes full of stress. For me, stress = shut down.

Knowing I'll touch something again also lets me put things into the box without having made a *final* decision. As a lover of all things procrastinative, I find it much easier to think, *I'll go ahead and put this in there and make the final decision later.*

Later. There's that delusional word again. In Later Land, I'm more decisive, more organized, and I can totally predict the future. A box full of almost-made-but-not-made decisions means every time I see the box, I have a nagging feeling the box holds something I should have kept. Nagging feelings are great reasons to stick the box on a shelf in the garage and wait for a better time to go through it again.

And if the pretty, reusable Donate Box sits on the shelf, future decluttering projects can't just be decluttering projects. They first have to be empty-the-box-full-of-nagging-feelings projects before I can start decluttering.

And that is another great excuse to procrastinate some more.

When the Donate Box is the bus instead of the bus stop, decisiveness is easier. There's relief in the deadline, in options being reduced to none. I like knowing that, once something is in the Donate Box, I'll never have to think about it again. Ever. A Donate Box that can't be donated is a Procrastination Station.

> When the Donate Box is the bus instead of the bus stop, decisiveness is easier.

Lest you complicate something that is as ridiculously simple as it sounds, let me clarify that a donatable Donate Box can be a trash bag, a shopping bag, a paper sack, a suitcase you're donating, or whatever. As long as it goes to the donation center along with the items inside, you're good.

My Feet

My feet are my most important decluttering tool. And the best part? I never lose them!

I use my feet to follow the "right now" part of Decluttering Question #1 (the part that isn't a question): "Take it there right now."

Because of my love of excessive efficiency, my former decluttering efforts went something like this: *Oh, this goes in the master bathroom. I'll make a master bathroom pile here. That goes in the playroom, so I'll make a playroom pile. These nails should be in the garage, so here's a garage pile.*

Six piles later, life happened. I left the decluttering project to go take care of life with every intention of coming back as soon as I could.

But I didn't.

Either more life happened, or I forgot. When I finally returned to the project a few hours (or a few days or a few months) later, those totally logical little piles had morphed into one big pile that was no longer the least bit sorted. The clutter that once drove me crazy while it sat behind the cabinet door or inside the drawer? Now it was out in the open, *outside the area I was decluttering.*

I'd created a bigger mess.

But if I take each individual item where it goes as soon as I answer "Where would I look for it first?" then at any point when I get distracted— not *if* I get distracted—whether I've decluttered one thing or twenty things, I've made progress.

Less stuff = decluttering progress. I might not be finished, but the space is better than it was when I started.

So while it seems more efficient to create piles now and take a delivery trip through the house later, it's not. That totally logical strategy doesn't work.

What's Not on the Supply List: A Keep Box

Did you notice what's *not* on the list of decluttering supplies? A Keep Box.

Keep Boxes don't work for me. At all.

Keep Boxes seem so logical, and they even prevent the pile-morphing issue. But in my world, they're not Keep Boxes. They're Procrastination Boxes, and my garage is full of them.

Remember how the purpose of a donatable Donate Box is to eliminate the halfway point? Keep Boxes are also halfway points. They are Procrastination Stations.

A Keep Box is a place to keep things I *think* I need. I *think* I need these things, but I don't have a clue where they should go. Keep Boxes let me tell myself I'll figure that out later. (And *later* is a bad word, remember?)

The beauty of the two (and only two) decluttering questions is if you answer either one, there's no need for a Keep Box. No need whatsoever. You're done. It's over.

One Last Excuse for Why This Won't Work

I can read your mind. I know what you're thinking. When I share my strategy for decluttering without making a bigger mess, I receive the same question over and over and over.

"But what do I do when I get distracted by another decluttering project? What if I 'take it there right now' and find the space where I'd look for it first is its own decluttering project ~~waiting~~ needing to happen?"

My entire house needed to be decluttered, so I get it. There wasn't one space bursting at the seams; the entire house was ready to burst. Everywhere I turned, I saw clutter.

So how did I get over this issue? Mostly, I just did. I got over it. I had to.

The more I decluttered, the more I realized telling myself I had to have a perfectly decluttered house wasn't helping. The top-to-bottom-or-what's-the-point mentality was detrimental to making progress. When I tackled one small space at a time, prioritizing by visibility and *just* decluttering instead of organizing, I began to see lasting change.

I choose the space I'm tackling for the day (or for the fifteen-minute period), and I work on *that* space at the expense of all other spaces. That space is my focus.

I use the two decluttering questions to make final decisions about everything I pull out of the pile/overstuffed drawer/can't-close-the-door closet. I'm working on *that* space. I don't have to worry about what I find when I take things where they go.

If I'm adding one more bottle of craft paint to a drawer full of jumbled up bottles of craft paint, that's okay. Putting away the one bottle of craft paint is my job at the moment. The paint drawer needs to be purged, straightened, and given an overall overhaul, but that is a project for another day. Today, if it's closeable, I close it. Once the drawer is closed, the mess is no longer visible.

This strategy isn't ideal, but a lot has to happen in my home before I get the luxury of doing what's ideal.

But sometimes there *isn't* any room for the thing I'm taking there right now. The place where I'd look for it first is overfull with stuff itself. I truly can't stick one more thing in there without everything toppling down.

I take a deep breath and follow the One-In-One-Out Rule. Remember this rule from the Container Concept? The clutter-busting strategy that seems obvious to everyone whose home isn't always a wreck but was far from obvious to me? If I need to put something away but there's no room, I have to take something else out to make room.

If I find a stapler in the bathroom drawer (it could happen) and take that stapler to the drawer where I keep office supplies, but the drawer is completely full, I don't have to stop and declutter office supplies. I only have to make room for the stapler. I choose one thing that deserves to be in the drawer less than the stapler does.

What do I remove? Easy stuff. Things that obviously need to go. If one easy thing doesn't make enough room, I remove a few easy things.

The last time I needed space in our office supply drawer, I found a large package of pencils, completely empty. All the pencils had fallen out and were scattered on the bottom of the drawer. I had seen the empty package before, but my brain hadn't identified it as trash. Instead, I thought, *Ugh. I need to find time to declutter my office supply drawer.*

But when I'm taking the stapler where it goes (right now), the office supply drawer is not my project. I am simply practicing the game-changing One-In-One-Out Rule. The empty box is easy and just happens to be about the size of a stapler.

Does more need to be done in that drawer? Definitely. Is now the time? No.

I head back to the original decluttering project with the empty pencil package in my hand, because I already have a trash bag or trash can there.

If I choose to remove something that I will donate, my Donate Box is back at the scene of my decluttering project as well.

I'm making progress. I'm not making a bigger mess.

. . . .

Proof It's Not Just Me

"I love the mess-free decluttering plan. I can't tell you how many times I've started, been interrupted, and ended up with bags that sat around adding to the clutter for weeks. Putting it away immediately seems like a waste of time and steps, but it keeps more clutter from happening. Oh, and I hate the advice of take everything out of a space and choose what goes back in—that advice ends up with multiple messes instead of one!"

—Penelope P.

"This whole idea that you could and should 'take it there right now' was totally mind-blowing and a complete game changer for me. I may not get quite as large a space decluttered or as big a pile cleaned up, *but* when it's done—it's done! No *new* pile to put away!"

—Linda S.

"When I started taking something there right away, my decluttering projects became less overwhelming. The stuff disappeared gradually, so by the end I didn't have dreaded piles to deal with. That's when all the excitement and steam has gone anyway—who wants to put away piles then and make the decision for a second time?"

—Stephanie T.

"The best thing I ever did was follow your advice about taking things to their spot right away. We have a big closet that gets stuffed with all my craft supplies, Christmas decorations, and out-of-season clothes. I cleaned it out recently, and instead of making piles of things in my dining room to go elsewhere, I took them where we would look for them, right then. Amazingly, it only took me half a day to get everything put back and cleaned up, and my dining room was able to be used that night! It used to stay stacked with stuff for days until I got around to putting it all away."

—Melissa H.

22

....

Head Explosions, Regret, and Re-decluttering

Fantasy: I have to declutter correctly. Why go through the trouble if I'm not going to do it right?

Reality: I'm going to spend the rest of my life decluttering. It's worth the trouble even if I'm terrible at it.

The Head Explosion Rule

Sometimes, even when I've made it through my two decluttering questions and know I need to stick something in the Donate Box, I just can't. I keep groaning and moaning and waffling.

I agonize.

What-ifs flood my brain. Yes. I'd look for (whatever it is) in a certain place. But I'd be mad I kept this particular one when I found it. Unless I was completely desperate. Then I might be happy to *at least* have this.

These feelings usually happen with *almost* wonderful things. Once upon a time, I loved this belt. Now, though, the belt is damaged or not my current style. I stare into space, trying to decide if I love it enough to take the time to undo the damage or update the style. Or I imagine a scenario in which my life might depend on this belt.

The shirt looks great on me, but I don't actually wear it. It has a teeny-tiny hole at the waist. These scissors technically cut, but I get mad every time I use them because they're rusted and hard to squeeze. I bought this soap dispenser because it matched my shower curtain, but I have to bang the pump so hard it bruises my hand.

I've made a rule. If I feel like my head is going to explode while deciding whether something is worth keeping, I don't keep it. I call it the Head Explosion Rule. No possibly-useful-but-not-actually-useful item is worth my head exploding.

It's just not. I choose the possibility of regret over dealing with the aftermath of an exploded head.

Decluttering Regret

Sometimes I'm wrong. Sometimes I get rid of an item and realize later I should have kept it. I thought I was being wise for throwing away a random screw I found on the living room floor. We're always finding random things like that, sticking them in a random place, and then never needing them again. The next day, we realized our newish recliner was broken. It had lost a screw.

Oops.

We have too many water bottles! How many do we really need? Umm, how about five? There are five of us, so why would we ever need more than that?

Then we invite friends to the pool, and they don't bring their own water bottles. Ugh. Maybe I should have kept a few extras.

I've made mistakes, and I've felt decluttering regret. Sometimes the regret is small; sometimes it's big. But every single time, I have survived. I can live without stuff. Since the beginning of the earth, people have gone through tough times, losing everything and coming back stronger than ever. I may get mad at myself over a bad decision, but as long as the people I love are safe, we're going to be okay.

Remember, people whose homes are always clutter-free prefer living with regret over living with clutter.

Re-decluttering

At times I don't follow the Head Explosion Rule. This happens less often now than when I started my deslobification process, but it does happen. I fret and worry over whether I should keep something and decide I just can't bear to part with it now.

A year later, I realize I was wrong, and that's perfectly okay.

Re-decluttering is a thing. Really. I didn't know it was a thing when I started my deslobification process. I thought I would eventually be done. I would reach a finish line where I had purged everything I didn't need from my home.

Those ~~assumptions~~ delusions made me think I had to declutter *correctly*. Perfectly. As a Project Person, I didn't want to redo my work.

I now know I'll never finish decluttering. With each season of life and every season of the year, new things come into my house, and old things turn into clutter.

I now find freedom in knowing I'll eventually re-declutter.

Re-decluttering will happen, and it's so much easier than decluttering. The first time I went through a space was hard. I was building my decluttering confidence, developing (and getting the hang of) my two decluttering questions. Petrified of making the wrong decision, I kept some things that caused me stress.

> People whose homes are always clutter-free prefer living with regret over living with clutter.

But a year (or two) later, when I re-declutter the same space, the angst is gone. I don't have as much stuff to go through because I decluttered last year. Things that stressed me out last time look completely different to me now. I remember the inner turmoil I felt over this pair of shoes, but now I feel nothing. A year has passed, and I haven't worn them once. I'm ready to donate, drama-free!

. . . .

Proof It's Not Just Me

"A conversation I have to have with myself is 'But you have so many memories associated with this, shouldn't you keep it for that?' (Jacqui the slob) 'But I hate those memories and don't want to remember them!' (Jacqui the declutterer) 'You can't just throw away memories; they made you who you are today.' (Jacqui the slob) 'Argh, just shut up; it's going!' (Jacqui the declutterer following the Head Explosion Rule!)"

—Jacqui K.

23

Sentimental Clutter

Fantasy: I love memories. I keep certain things because they remind me of a person or a place, and I cherish those memories.

Reality: I keep things. All kinds of things. I default to keeping them because they might hold a memory.

As I've worked through my own clutter and experienced life within my Clutter Threshold, I've become less sentimental about things. I used to think every card I received, every photo I developed, every word my children wrote was sentimental.

Now I realize holding so many things dear devalues the things that are truly special memories. If a treasured memory is buried in a pile of clutter, I'm not honoring it.

Let me be clear. I won't pretend I understand the attachment someone feels to certain things after experiencing a traumatic event. I'm not a psychologist, and I've never lost a child. Even typing those words, I feel panic rising in my chest, so I know I can't possibly imagine the reality of your grief if you have experienced that.

Take these ideas for what they are. They're words from someone who knows how it feels to be suffocated by the stuff in her home and who has experienced the relief that comes with having less stuff and more room to live. I've decluttered things I once believed I could never declutter. I've experienced both regret and joy over my decluttering decisions.

Keep One

Less is better. Less inspires me to keep decluttering.

I grieve with the passage of each stage of life. I even grieve at the end of each summer. I've learned to identify the melancholy/panicky feeling that comes over me in August as I watch my kids playing in the pool and wonder how much they'll change before next summer. Will they still want to swim every day? Will they look forward to seeing the same friends? Will my son finally have the hairy armpits he so desperately wants?

As my children pass through each stage of life, I find myself wanting to hang on to things that remind me of that stage. I've learned, however, that the memories come rushing back when I see one tiny outfit. I don't need to see every outfit to remember how little they were.

I kept one favorite 0–3 month outfit for each of my kids. I didn't choose the outfits they wore when they came home from the hospital; I chose my favorites. The outfits that bring back the most memories. The ones that make me smile the most.

> Feeling happy is better than feeling overwhelmed.

The three tiny outfits I chose make me happy. The boxes and boxes of clothes that I kept for way too long and tripped over in my garage overwhelmed me. Feeling happy is better than feeling overwhelmed.

I kept three tiny pairs of cowboy boots. My boys wore them everywhere one year—with shorts, to the zoo, with their pajamas. Those boots remind me that their adult-sized feet were once tiny and kissable. I don't need every sock and sandal they ever wore to see those little toes in my mind's eye.

Don't Assume You Know What's in the Box

I grieve over my own passing life phases. In my thirties, I came across an old Keep Box full of papers and books from my college days. I assumed the box was full of memories. When I actually went through it, though, I realized more than half of the papers were blank or full of scribbled notes I couldn't even read. I only cared about one or two papers I remember staying up all night to write. A few textbooks produced fond memories, but most didn't bring back any memories at all. Once I actually looked through the box, purging more than half of its contents was easy.

Less was easy.

Feel the Pain

No one likes pain, but sometimes it's necessary. Parting with sentimental clutter is legitimately painful. But if this stuff is keeping my family from living comfortably in our home, it needs to go.

I felt sick to my stomach and short of breath when I helped a woman load our baby crib into the back of her pickup truck. Knowing our baby years were over was painful.

I don't regret selling the crib. Thinking about selling the crib and watching it go was painful, but the joy and peace of a less-cluttered home makes it worth the temporary pain I experienced in the moment of separation.

Designate a Container

When I was a child, on a family weekend trip, my mother purchased a metal box at an antique store in the little town of Jefferson, Texas. We called it my Jefferson Box, and I used it to store my most precious things.

I loved that box. When I wanted to keep something safe, my mother told me to put it in my Jefferson Box.

I knew the Jefferson Box held special memories, but as a budding slob, I didn't know it was a container. (I didn't know what a container was.)

I see now that my mother's idea was brilliant. She gave me a space, a limited space, to keep and protect my childhood treasures.

One of my college roommates occasionally pulls out her Theatre Box when we get together. She has copies of playbills, pictures of us in costumes, and random mementos she took home after the last performance of a favorite show.

I love looking at her box. I have many similar things, but I have no idea where they are. They're probably scattered throughout random boxes in my attic. I'm sure many have been lost.

Her Theatre Box achieves several purposes. It limits the number of mementos she can keep, making her sort out the less-significant ones. It protects the things she does keep. The box keeps her mementos all together so she can easily look through them when she's in the mood to relive those fun years of her life.

She treasures those items.

If an item is truly sentimental, truly impossible to purge, that item should be treasured.

Get Professional Help

As I said in the beginning of this chapter, I'm not a psychologist. I'm not a therapist. I'm not a voice of experience for true grief or grief recovery. If your grief is paralyzing you while your abundance of stuff suffocates you, please get professional help. Asking for help is not a sign of weakness; it's a sign that you have the strength to do what you need to do. Search the Internet for grief recovery groups at churches near you, or ask your doctor to recommend someone who can help.

Just like there are real steps to getting rid of your clutter, there are steps to walking through your grief.

24

Clutter Guilt

Fantasy: I have a gift. A unique gift for appreciating all things cool, potentially useful, historical, or sentimental. Or valuable. Or beautiful. Or quirky. People recognize this quality in me and trust me with their treasures, knowing I will value them as they deserve to be valued.

Reality: I like stuff. I have an overactive imagination about the potential value of stuff and about my ability to fix or sell or use or arttully display this stuff. People see me as a dumping ground. They can get rid of their own junk without feeling any guilt because they know I'll be excited to take it.

Clutter guilt is a real thing. It can be self-imposed or imposed by others, but both words are bad words. *Clutter* is stuff I don't need. *Guilt* is something I feel when I have done something bad or (even worse) *feel* like I've done something bad *even when I haven't*.

Clutter guilt is a bad thing. Period.

Why Clutter Guilt Doesn't Deserve to Be a Thing (Even Though It Totally Is)

My home is *my* home. It's *my* space. Anyone who isn't living in (or paying for) my space doesn't have a say in what I keep in it.

The living in/paying for clarification is necessary because I'm only talking about stuff that is truly mine. I'm not talking about stuff that's driving me crazy but that my husband insists we keep. That's not clutter guilt. That's clutter irritation. They're different, and I'll talk about dealing with other people's clutter in an upcoming chapter.

I'm also not talking about getting rid of stuff Uncle Harry stores in the closets of his house that you're living in rent-free. Or the stuff you agreed to keep for your cousin while she moved to Africa for a year. (Is that enough qualifying mumbo jumbo to help you understand what I'm actually talking about?)

I'm talking about *my* stuff. Stuff that's mine but that used to belong to someone else. I've collected it over the years because people "passed it on" or "thought I'd love to have it" or gave it to me for Christmas and will ask next year if I've enjoyed it.

It's my stuff, but someone else's feelings are attached to it.

This is my home, and I need to live in my home. If I can't sit down for a meal at my dinner table, I'm not living. If boxes are piled up in areas where I'm embarrassed to have boxes piled up, I'm not living.

> Living is sitting down. Living is moving through a room without tripping or turning sideways.

Living is sitting down. Living is moving through a room without tripping or turning sideways.

You know all this. Knowing this is the reason you're reading this book. You've worked your way through the easy stuff, developed habits that are making an impact, and purged a lot already. Now, you're ready to deal with the stuff that makes your stomach hurt.

External Clutter Guilt

Let's start with clutter guilt placed on you by others. This one is easiest for me because it gets my you-can't-tell-me-what-to-do inner-fourteen-year-old going. I hate this stuff, but I keep it because I feel bad about disappointing the person who gave it to me. If it wasn't for Aunt Clara, I wouldn't think twice about sending that ceramic pineapple to the thrift store.

Here is the logical approach: if they don't want this stuff in their own home, they shouldn't expect me to keep it in mine.

I mean, duh. They decluttered it. They get to enjoy *not* having it in their house. I get to do the same thing.

But family dynamics come into play when getting rid of guilt clutter, and it's not that easy. While my number one recommended method is to donate now and play dumb later, there are other ways not to trample on family members' feelings.

Stop Being the Family Dumping Ground

Let's be honest. You're an easy target. If you're like me, you used to love getting all the family treasures. Your face *would* light up at the box full of bills Grandma paid during the Great War. There was a time when you couldn't understand why no one else in the family wanted that box!

But now you know about your Clutter Threshold. The clutter dumping has to stop.

Here's one approach: send a family e-mail telling people to come get what they want, rent a Dumpster, and throw it all away in one weekend. That's a valid approach, and it has definite merits. But because it's exactly the type of advice someone would give who has never struggled with irrational feelings of attachment to a plastic giraffe, I'll share some additional thoughts.

The slow-cooker decluttering approach (the approach that produces a homey home without anyone sizzling from the burn) starts with saying no to the people who continually declutter their own homes guilt-free by blessing you with junk they don't want.

Say no to new stuff these people bring you. Stopping them won't be easy, but it must be done. Ironically, these same declutterers often lay on the most intense clutter guilt.

Say no. Or "No, thank you." Practice right now. "No, thank you." Go to the mirror, say it again, and respond to yourself with the face Aunt Iggy will make when she hears you tell her no. She'll be shocked. Raise your eyebrows and drop your jaw and show the bewilderment in your eyes.

The conversation is not going to be easy, but you *can* say, "No, thank you." When she pretends not to hear you, say, "No, thank you!" louder. When she counters with "But it'll look great in your kitchen!" say, "No, thank you" again.

Don't explain. Stick to the facts. You don't want it, so "no" is all you need to say.

If you have to keep talking (I understand because I'm an excessive explainer), say, "I'm trying to get clutter out of my house, so I can't bring anything else in right now."

Be honest. I don't know why honesty is extra hard with family, but as with everything else, it's the best policy. Be honest that you are struggling. Be honest that you've realized taking this kind of stuff is one of the reasons your home is a mess. Ignore her knowing eyes and annoyingly exuberant nod and attempts to turn the conversation to a discussion of your housekeeping failures.

Over time, she'll give up. Or at least she'll give up a little sooner in the here-ya-go-no-thanks-please-take-it-I-really-don't-want-it conversation.

You have trained people to view you as the place they can dump their own guilt clutter guilt-free. You need time to retrain them.

If someone won't take no for an answer, tell her you'll drop off her treasures at a donation center as a favor to her. If she sticks the clutter in your trunk, go straight to the donation center.

If Aunt Iggy is horrified you took her ceramic pineapple to a donation center, widen your eyes in surprise and remind her you said that was what you were going to do before she put it in your trunk.

Resisting the guilters' clutter advances will have two positive effects. You'll avoid future decluttering, and you'll be getting them ready for what is coming next: getting rid of the stuff they guilted you into taking in the past.

The Physical Reaction Test

Getting rid of guilt-laced clutter is never easy, but let's approach it the same way you approached the other clutter in your home. Start with the easy stuff. The easy stuff in the guilt category is the stuff you hate. These things produce a physical sense of loathing. They make your ears feel warm and your scalp tingle. If you hate something, it has no place in your home, no matter how much someone else thought you should appreciate it.

If you are too scared to donate now and explain later, try the method you've been using to avoid clutter gifts: honesty.

You've realized you were only keeping the ceramic pineapple out of worry for the giver's feelings, and you now see that's not a valid reason for holding on to clutter. You have a Clutter Threshold, and this set of teacups exceeds your personal threshold. They make you feel panicky and resentful. You want these treasures to go to someone who will appreciate them the way they deserve to be appreciated.

Aunt Betsy won't have a clue what you're talking about, but your passionate rambling will show you've put a great deal of thought into getting rid of this stuff.

Explain that while you wish you had a knack for decorating and could create a beautiful display of Grandma's spoon collection, you don't have that knack. The spoons don't fit your decor as they are, so they've been in a box for years. Those spoons deserve to come out of the box and make someone happy!

As someone who suffers from excessive honesty, I'll tell you that most people, while surprised, react well to honesty. Being honest that you don't have a place for this in your home takes the blame (something no one responds well to) off them and puts the responsibility on you without you actually keeping the item.

One last thing before we move into other kinds of clutter guilt: let

Granny see you're getting rid of all sorts of stuff. You are purging clothes, shoes, furniture, and your own childhood memories. Her personal treasures (things she claims to value even though she didn't want them in her own home) didn't make the cut. You didn't suddenly decide to start hating her and all the things she's ever given you; you're just decluttering.

Imaginary Clutter Guilt

While most families have a clutter gifter and clutter guilt can be a very real thing, it can also be imaginary. The only way you're going to find out if your clutter guilt is imaginary is to ask the person you think is going to hate you forever. Just don't ask this question: "Do you mind if I get rid of _____?" Ask this one instead: "Do you want _____ back? I'm getting rid of it." That follow-up statement, "I'm getting rid of it," is key. Do not leave that statement out. You're not asking for permission to get rid of it. You're giving them the chance to rescue it before you donate. It's their house or the thrift store. Those are the only two options.

Here's what I've learned from my own experience: usually, the guilt-tripper isn't as worried as the guilt-trippee thinks he/she is.

Self-Imposed Clutter Guilt

Some clutter guilt has nothing to do with pressure from other people, but comes from your own obsession with sending your stuff to a place where it will be loved and appreciated in the way you're no longer able to love and appreciate it.

Stressing over the "best" way of doing something is totally counterproductive if that stress keeps you from doing anything at all.

I'm going to tell you something that makes me feel a little bit bad but that I've decided *not* to feel guilty about.

I don't donate to my church's garage sales.

What? A church garage sale is a prime decluttering opportunity! Good cause, free pickup, great motivation to declutter with a deadline . . . what's not to love?

They don't take clothing.

Because I now live a lifestyle of decluttering, decluttering all year long, I always have a Donate Box or three going. But I don't sort. Once something is in the Donate Box, I'm done. I've already decided it's leaving my home. I will not go back through my boxes of already-made-decisions to remove clothing.

Once upon a time, I sorted my clutter. I thought I was being wise and practical, but I was placing unnecessary stress on myself. Unnecessary stress = a really good reason not to start decluttering.

I made a pile of things I'd been given. I tried to think of someone to whom I could give these hand-me-downs that were given to me.

I made another pile of things I'd purchased or been given as gifts. (Gifts are different from hand-me-downs on my complicated can-I-sell-it-or-not internal checklist.) Actually, that was two piles. I separated things that were perfect enough to sell on eBay from items with small flaws that I could put in a garage sale.

Want to guess what happened next?

The bag of second-time-around-hand-me-downs went into my car, if I was lucky. Usually, I placed it near the door to wait until the next time I knew I'd see so-and-so. *I couldn't possibly forget to take this bag to my friend if I put the bag by the door.* After weeks (or months) of forgetting, I *might* remember to take the bag to a playdate and offer the clothes to anyone who wanted them.

The eBayable items went to my eBay room, where they waited until the right time to sell. The garage sale stuff went to the garage. I waited until I had enough other stuff, until the weather was going to be nice, and until we had nothing else going on so we could devote a weekend (and the week before) to having a sale.

I'm grateful I no longer live in that world. Did you notice all my clutter-sorting scenarios involved the word "wait" in some form? Like coffee mugs in the sink or scissors in a Keep Box, anything that involves stuff moving *temporarily* creates a Procrastination Station. I can't have Procrastination Stations in my home.

Now, I bring my current donatable Donate Box into the room where I'm decluttering. Even if it is full of pots and pans and I'm purging my sock drawer, I fill it up. When I'm done, I stick it in the donate spot. When I get a notice in the mail that someone is picking up ~~junk~~ donations, I haul my current Donate Box(es) out to my front porch. If/when I miss a few of those pickups, I call someone to come get it or load the boxes in my Suburban and take it somewhere that accepts all of my stuff. Everything. Together.

Guilt-free.

> Like coffee mugs in the sink or scissors in a Keep Box, anything that involves stuff moving *temporarily* creates a Procrastination Station. I can't have Procrastination Stations in my home.

I shan't sort again. Ever. Sorting adds time and angst and oh-so-many excuses to the decluttering process, and all those things add up to a strange type of self-imposed clutter guilt.

Proof It's Not Just Me

"I have a very well-intentioned friend who constantly drops over bags of 'stuff.' I thought I'd gotten through to her, but when I got home from work, I found an old, yellowed quilt sitting at my front door. So I donated it to an animal shelter.

"She asked me where the quilt was, and I told her I had regifted it. I was met with a stony silence and a pair of raised eyebrows, but I haven't had any mystery parcels dropped off since, and she is still talking to me, so maybe, just maybe, she finally heard me?"

—Anonymous

25

The Value Trap: Sell or Donate?

Fantasy: I've got a lot of stuff, but some of this stuff is worth money. I know I need to declutter, but one of these days, I'm going to figure out how and where to sell these things. I bet there's something in here that could pay for a vacation!

Reality: I've got a lot of stuff. Once I finally get around to selling something, I usually realize I've been hanging on to stuff I don't even like for a very long time, just to sell it in a garage sale for a quarter.

Perceived (or imagined) monetary value is one of the most difficult decluttering trip-ups. Let me be clear: anything you truly love or that makes you happy or makes your life easier has value. But if you are holding on to something you think is worth money—even though you don't like it, use it, or have room for it—you need to get rid of it.

Two options allow me to stay under my personal Clutter Threshold:

Option #1: Sell things.

Option #2: Give things away.

Not an Option in Any Way, Shape, or Form: Keep something, even though I hate it, because I *think* it *might* be worth money.

I once viewed every object in my home according to its resale value. I spent huge amounts of time and energy milking every possible dollar out of my clutter. Decluttering that way meant junk I didn't want continued cluttering my home long after the moment I decided I didn't want it anymore. Now, I almost always donate. But if you're coming from the place where I started, I know telling you to just donate it all would make you throw this book across the room.

Instead, I'm telling you to be realistic, and I'm sharing the various ways to sell your stuff along with the effort required for each so you can figure out what might actually happen in your home. If my experience helps you get your stuff out faster, I'll have succeeded.

Determining the True Value of Your Treasures

Many a knickknack fanatic has dreamed of making lots of money from her collections.

There's no need to let the somewhat foggy idea of how much money you *might* get for something keep you from decluttering. Clear the fog right now. Sometimes, the best way to part with an item you've always believed to be valuable is to find out it's not.

You can use eBay to learn the current market value of Grandma's porcelain frog collection within five minutes.

Grab a frog. Turn it over. Type what you see into the search bar on eBay.com. Are the pictures exactly the same as the frog you have in your hand? Don't get excited yet. The first thing you'll see is what other people selling this item think it's worth.

Maybe they know what they're talking about. Maybe they don't.

I've been there. My heart does a little flip when I see someone selling the exact same thing I have for $150! Except on the first page of search results, they're not. They're *trying* to sell the exact same thing for $150. Scroll down and look on the left-hand side of the page. Look for two words: *Completed listings*. Completed listings matter. Nothing else does in your search for reality.

The main (difficult) lesson I learned in my eBay days is that an item is only worth what someone is willing to pay for it. The completed listings page is your reality check page. I've felt my excitement deflate when I realized no one (even in the worldwide marketplace of eBay) was willing to spend even a few dollars on the treasures I once believed would pay for my kids' braces.

With a five-minute reality check, you'll either learn your treasure isn't worth what you though it was, or you'll have a realistic idea of how much you could get for it if you put in the effort required to get that money.

So let's talk about the reality of that effort.

What Is Involved in Selling on eBay?

First, you have to research. Is your item an original or a replica? Is it flawed? Has it been altered from its original state? Is it exactly like the one that sold in the completed listings?

Next, you'll photograph the item, upload the photos, and create the listing (writing a detailed description that clearly states all flaws or special features). If it sells, you'll wait for payment, pack it (carefully, so it doesn't break), and ship it.

Is the money you can expect to get worth all of that? Can you even "expect" to get that much? If some items like yours didn't sell at all, there is a chance you'll do the work for nothing.

If you're willing to risk your time and money, check one more thing before you sell: shipping costs. Find the box you would use, and calculate the shipping with the dimensions of the box (not the dimensions of the item; there's usually a big difference) and the weight of the item plus packing materials plus the box.

Think I'm going overboard? I have *many* stories of mistakes I made on eBay, but I'll share just one. A few years ago (long after I'd stopped selling regularly), I bought a Halloween costume at a garage sale for the sole purpose of selling it on eBay. I had checked completed listings on my phone and found others exactly like it selling for fifteen and twenty dollars.

I couldn't resist.

I knew better, but I started the auction at ninety-nine cents. The costume sold for ninety-nine cents. With fees from eBay and PayPal, and only very slightly underestimating shipping costs, I lost money. I didn't calculate the cost of the envelope or the gas I used to drive to the post office. I don't even want to talk about the value of my time or the fifty cents I spent on the costume.

I went through a lot of hassle and spent about three dollars of my own money to get a stranger in another state a great deal on a Halloween costume.

Have you noticed a theme? Selling on eBay is work, and sometimes that work doesn't even pay off. You'll work hard for every dime you earn.

Selling Online Without Shipping

If you've decided eBay is too much trouble but are still determined to sell, there are other ways to sell online that don't involve the hassle of shipping. Craigslist and local Facebook swap groups are other options for selling online.

You'll describe and share pictures of the items you want to sell, and people will let you know if they are interested. Because you won't have to ship, selling breakable or large items is easier. But because you meet the buyer in person, safety is of utmost importance. Meeting at a public location in daylight is a good idea but can be a hassle. Loading a big item into your vehicle and then unloading it five minutes later at the safe location only to help Mr. Stranger load it into *his* vehicle? Kind of a pain.

Setting up meeting times is also a hassle. This usually involves multiple back-and-forth e-mails between you and a buyer. Sometimes, even after answering multiple questions, people flake and tell you they don't want it or simply stop responding to your e-mails. You start again with the next person who desperately wanted it, but she tells you she's changed her mind.

When selling this way works, it's great. When it doesn't, it's annoying. Either way, time and hassle are involved.

Consignment Sales or Selling to Resellers

If the idea of selling things yourself overwhelms you to the point that it's never actually going to happen but you're still not ready to donate, call local specialty resellers. Look up "furniture consignment" or "sports equipment resale" in your area. Call, tell them what you have, and ask if they will buy from you or sell on consignment.

If you have large numbers of smaller items, there are people who will sell things for you and take a portion of the money. Ask your local friends where they consign their kids' clothing, furniture, baby stuff, etc., or search online for websites that do this.

Selling by consignment can be great because you drop off (or ship) your stuff and get paid immediately or when the items sell. In reality, there's still work involved. Many consignment stores and websites only take things in perfect condition, and some only take high-end brands. So you'll have to sort and carefully examine your stuff. Many also require that clothing be ironed and hanging on a certain type of hanger.

Learn the requirements before you go through the hassle of hauling your stuff somewhere. I've spoken with *many* people who tried to consign things, only to have less than a third of their offerings accepted.

If you have high value items, an antique store or antiquities dealer might be your best option. Again, they take their cut but do the majority of the work involved. Ask friends who have successfully used people in your area for recommendations to avoid involvement with unscrupulous characters.

Still too much hassle?

Have a Garage Sale

We started with the strategy that has the potential to earn the most, but requires the most hassle, and have moved to the method that will earn less money for individual items, but requires less-detailed effort.

A garage sale is your last resort for making money. But if you've ever had one, you probably think I'm crazy to put it lower down on the hassle scale.

A garage sale is a *lot* of work, but it is not where you'll earn top dollar for each individual item you sell. People expect to pay "garage sale prices" at garage sales. Don't look on eBay and think someone will pay that price while she's sweating on your driveway, digging through boxes of onesies. You are not setting up a resale boutique in your garage. Price as low as you possibly can so people will leave carrying as much of your clutter with them as humanly possible.

The reduced-hassle advantage of this lower-class sales venue comes from the lack of detail required to sell individual items. If an item is slightly dented but still perfectly usable, a garage sale shopper can determine its usability for herself. She's the one responsible for examining closely before she buys. You stick it on a table and open your garage.

Most important, there is no "if it doesn't sell" tactic after a garage sale. You've already given the higher-earning ways a shot, or you've decided they're not worth your time. Decide ahead of time that anything you don't sell will not reenter your home. Knowing you'll donate the dog crate if it doesn't sell at your garage sale will make you willing to take less for it. You'll end up with more money and less clutter than you had when you started.

No Money, No Hassle—Donate

Last, but definitely not least, donate. Donate wherever to whomever. Donate to your favorite cause or the person who happens to ask at the right time. I donate to anyone who will come to my house and doesn't make me sort.

If you live in the United States and donate to a qualifying organization, you can get a receipt for your donations to use for a tax deduction.

Whatever You Do, Get Clutter Out of Your House

You bought this book to learn how to get your house in order, not to learn how to be a millionaire. The point of this chapter wasn't to tell you how to get the most money out of your excess stuff. My goal was to help you bust through your perceived value excuse, a favorite excuse for people like me.

Maybe your stuff *is* valuable and you *do* need the money. If that's the case, sell it. Get the money you need while getting clutter out of your house.

Living miserably, surrounded by clutter while believing you could get a lot of money if you just knew how, is not an option.

If this chapter made you groan and confirmed you'll never actually go through the hassle of selling, donate.

I've been through each of these steps and can say with confidence that donating is the very best way (the easiest, the fastest, the least stressful) for me to get clutter out of my house.

> Living miserably, surrounded by clutter while believing you could get a lot of money if you just knew how, is not an option.

One More Thing to Get Over

If you don't want to go through the hassle of making a direct connection with the exact person who can't wait to buy what you don't want (through eBay, Craigslist, a garage sale, etc.), someone else is going to make money selling your stuff.

If you are not personally selling an item to someone who personally wants that item, you will not get the full value, and you don't deserve the full value. The middleman will get his cut for the work he does.

I once dragged a large plastic tub full of heavy books to a used bookstore. A woman scanned my books, punched a few keys on her computer, and told me the store would give me more than forty dollars. I was thrilled. Walking out with cash in my hand and an empty tub was exciting. I went home and loaded up more books.

After driving around with the second batch of books in my trunk for a few months, I remembered to stop at the bookstore again. I was excited to see how much money I would get this time.

They offered me less than two dollars.

I was shocked. The cashier explained the system. The computer program predicts what they can sell and how much someone will pay for it.

Out of ~~principle~~ spite, I retrieved several of my "more valuable" books from my batch and left. The Spite Books sat in my trunk for another year (or so). My hopes for cash had been dashed, and I was embarrassed that someone was telling me these things I'd held on to for so long were worthless.

I'm over it now. (Mostly.) I'm not sure what was different about the two sets of books, but that's the point. *I didn't know.* The store's system knew because someone (whom they paid) had created a complex computer program that collected data from sales in their stores across the country. In each store, they pay for rent, electricity, and employees. Their business wouldn't succeed if they paid top dollar for things they could never sell.

They were the ones being realistic. They did the work. I just hauled in a box of stuff I didn't want.

I've now decided I don't care who sells my stuff. I just want it out of my house.

Don't get worked up over someone reselling your stuff. Either do the work to get the price you want, let someone give you money for taking your clutter, or give it away and stop worrying about it.

Just don't keep it in your house.

26

Decluttering Momentum

Fantasy: If I'm going to declutter, I need to start with the thing that's been plaguing me the most for the longest time.

Reality: The thing that plagues me the most is the hardest decision I need to make. If I wait to start until I can make that decision, I'll never start.

I love speaking to groups of women about home management and decluttering. I love seeing their eyes light up when people start to feel inspired about living with less.

But I get one question (in different forms) every time I speak.

Moms: What do I do about baby stuff when I don't know if I'm going to have more kids?

Teachers: I taught third grade for years, but now I'm teaching fifth. What do I do with my third grade stuff since I don't know if I'll need it again?

Quilters: My fabric stash is out of control, but it's so hard to get rid of anything since I never know when I'll need it. What do I do?

Here's the real question: I'm overwhelmed because I can't predict the future regarding the most important thing in my life, so what should I do?

My answer: I can't predict the future either. No one can. I definitely can't predict *your* future because it has nothing to do with me.

My solution: Don't start with difficult things. Do the easy stuff first.

You're almost finished with a book about getting your house under control. You're feeling hope. You might even be (as strange as it seems) excited about getting started, about finding your Clutter Threshold and being able to close your underwear drawer.

This excitement brings to mind the decluttering decision that stresses you most.

This decision, when you finally make it, will be emotional and difficult. When you purge that particular pile, you'll declare the end of an era in your life.

Don't start there. Don't even think about that stuff right now. Grab a trash bag. Do the easiest of the easy stuff.

When you feel inspired to declutter, your brain immediately focuses on the overwhelming decluttering decision that's been bugging you for months.

If I start with the most-overwhelming space in my home, I get overwhelmed and am a ba-jillion times more likely not to even start.

Make your kitchen more usable. Clear your dining room table and the top of the piano. Clear the floor of the laundry room.

Deal with nonemotional clutter first. Improve your home, live with those improvements, and something strange will happen: decluttering momentum.

When I started decluttering like a madwoman, I felt pain each time I purged. As a lifelong keeper, every hair bow and spatula and book entering the Donate Box felt like I was ripping out a little piece of my soul.

But I've changed. I have experience.

When my kids were little, I kept every piece of paper that had even a splash of their creative juices on it. The thought of not keeping a handout or a worksheet never even crossed my mind. My default decision was to stick them all in a stack to deal with later. As I decluttered my home and worked my way through pile after pile of mostly meaningless paper, saving only one special piece for every thirty or forty that were obviously trash, I began to view each paper that entered my home differently. My kids learned that there was no reason to keep math worksheets for posterity.

Over time, I've turned into a ruthless declutterer. I'm ruthless because I've experienced less, and I love having less stuff in my house. I love not bumping into things. I love offering my game room to someone who needs a place to sleep. I love being able to reach into my cabinet and grab the container I need without lids and bowls falling on my head.

I value open, livable space more than I value my stuff.

If I have another child after I've sold my baby stuff, I can buy someone else's baby things for significantly less than the value of the space that was clear and livable for two years.

If I teach third grade again, someone who has moved to fifth or just retired will be glad for *her* third grade stuff to be used.

If I need navy blue gingham for a quilt, I'll have a wonderful excuse to take a day trip with a friend to the quilt shop that's next door to my favorite tearoom.

I know life will go on, and I know I will survive. I know from experience. Get that experience with stuff that doesn't take your breath away.

Part 4

Change That Lasts

27

....

Other People

Fantasy: My house would be spotless if I didn't have to deal with the messes made by all these Other People who live here.

Reality: Even if that fantasy were true (which it's totally not), life wouldn't be very fun. I like these people.

I've forfeited the blame game.

This surrender has been a big part of my deslobification process. I could sound noble and say it was a conscious decision to accept responsibility for my own actions, but honestly, the forfeit just happened.

When I started the blog, I was confident I would fail. I had failed every other time I'd tried to change my messy ways.

My husband knew I wanted a blog, and he was all for it. He is *always* all for my crazy schemes. (Except for buying shelves.) I'd talked about my desire to have a blog for a year and a half. Eighteen months of dreaming and researching and putting it off because my house was a wreck.

But when I finally started *A Slob Comes Clean*, I didn't tell him. For the first six weeks or so, he had no idea I had a blog. I wasn't hiding it because I feared criticism. I hid what I was doing because it probably wasn't going to work.

I didn't tell my mother or my best friend or anyone except the faceless strangers on the Internet, none of whom were actually reading the blog yet. I set up the blog using a fake name (Nony, short for Anonymous) and set up a new e-mail address so no one I knew would ever trace these embarrassing confessions back to me.

I kept what I was doing a secret out of fear, but there was a bonus effect. Because I couldn't talk about what I was doing, I couldn't expect anyone to care. Or join me. Or help.

I was blathering on in cyberspace but keeping my physical mouth shut. With my mouth closed, I did the dishes. I worked it out in my brain through writing but not by boring those around me (like I'd done every other time I'd decided to change my messy ways).

Because I couldn't talk about what I was doing, two things happened. First, I only focused on, worked on, and analyzed what *I* was doing and what *I* wasn't doing. Through *only* what *I* was doing, the house started getting better. So much better. I made *huge* improvements without anyone realizing I was making huge improvements.

In the past, I'd try a new method. I'd tell the family my plan, and they'd nod. And forget. They didn't care like I did because they weren't the ones who'd noticed a problem and decided to change.

If I declared to the family we were no longer going to be messy, and then someone put a dirty dish in my sink, it felt personal. I had *told* them we weren't doing that anymore. I interpreted their lack of concern about dishes in the sink as a lack of love and appreciation for me. But because this time I hadn't told them what I was trying to do, I just moved the dish into the dishwasher without feeling rejected or unloved or unappreciated.

When the thought occurred to me in the right moment (thoughts don't often occur in the right moment for me), I asked/told (asked Hubby, told the kids) to put their dishes straight in the dishwasher. By this time, they had seen me loading the dishwasher every night, so my request made sense.

And I realized something: I had established routines by not establishing routines. When I asked my family to do something I hadn't been doing myself, they were confused. Things worked a certain way in our home. It was the complete opposite of how I *wanted* things to work, but it was all my kids knew.

Once I established routines for myself, my family could jump into those routines because the routines existed.

I compare it to an escalator. If you walk up to an escalator and it stops, then starts again, then speeds up, then goes slowly, you're not going to step on.

Even though escalators are slightly scary (don't you think?), people are willing to step on because they know exactly what is going to happen when they take the first step.

Once there was a routine, my family could jump in on the routine.

> I had established routines by not establishing routines. When I asked my family to do something I hadn't been doing myself, they were confused.

Accept Responsibility

Before we married, my husband kept a clean-for-a-bachelor apartment for years. He lived in a total mess only after he married me.

He knew how to do laundry. He knew how to wash dishes. He makes an awesome pancake breakfast on Saturday mornings.

He was always willing to help, but helping was a guessing game. He had to analyze the erratic situation and guess which household task would be most helpful. He'd run a load of laundry or load the dishwasher, but it wouldn't make a dent in the overall mess. His effort created no lasting effect, because it wasn't part of a routine—*because there wasn't a routine*. I didn't carry through on any progress he made.

With each helpful task that didn't help very much, his motivation to do the next helpful task died a little.

And he accepted a messy house as our normal.

I set the tone. I created our normal. I established our lack of routine.

But once I started doing the dishes, and *by* doing the dishes (rather than talking about doing the dishes) came up with a routine that worked for our home, he noticed the difference.

Now he starts the dishwasher as often as I do, because that's our routine. He knows if the dishwasher runs each night, our kitchen stays under control, and we don't end up eating cereal out of measuring cups.

He knows Monday is Laundry Day. He knows if we sort all our dirty clothes into piles on Sunday night, he'll (almost certainly) have clean socks every day for work.

The kids know what a five-minute pickup is. The first time we did it, I wanted to pull my hair out, but the second one was a little better. And the third was better than that. Now we've done countless five-minute pickups, and they're actually helpful. But I had to teach them.

Instead of throwing my hands in the air after the first unsuccessful attempt, I had to accept responsibility for the fact that they didn't know this. They didn't know where to put things because they'd never seen what our house was supposed to look like unless we were having a party. They had no idea what a clean-on-a-Wednesday living room should look like in our home.

The Big Clutter Log in My Own Eye

I'll tell you the stories of two pieces of clothing.

The first is a pair of navy blue gym shorts. The elastic is stretched and a little crackly. Paint spatters cover one side. The waistband is barely attached to the shorts, with more holes than thread.

The second is a T-shirt with thin, alternating stripes in two shades of green. The collar is barely attached to the rest of the shirt. A series of holes cascades down the back.

The gym shorts are mine. I keep them because they have a story. When I was a teacher in Bangkok, our school flooded during rainy season. The students stayed home that day, but teachers helped with the cleanup. We arrived in our dresses, so the PE teacher (my roommate) sold us all PE uniforms. It was an amazingly fun day in a unique and fleeting period of my life. I love those shorts because of that memory. When I look at them, I remember that day.

The T-shirt belongs to my husband. I think it's from a camp somewhere, but I really don't know.

I know the story of my gym shorts. It's my story, so I feel the feelings that make me keep it. The wear and tear is a visual reminder of the passage of time.

His shirt isn't my story, so I don't feel anything when I look at it. I just see the holes.

Years ago, I threw that green-striped T-shirt in the trash, and he pulled it back out. Like most wives would be, I was annoyed.

Now, it sits in his T-shirt drawer. As long as that drawer can close, who cares if a holey T-shirt sits in the bottom?

An Eye Full of Clutter Logs

My husband empties his pockets at the end of the day. Receipts, memos, and other randomness end up in a drawer by his bathroom sink.

The trash drawer used to drive me crazy. Why? It's *his* stuff.

My own randomness covers the dining room table (significantly more abundant and seen by random doorbell ringers), but it's mine. I know (pretty much) what is in the pile, and when I'll deal with it (maybe), and what needs to be done (for the most part).

His pile is out of my control, and even though it's significantly smaller than mine (or my many others throughout the house), being out of *my* control makes me view the pile as out of control, so it gets on my nerves.

Even when the entire house is out of control, I focus on *his* pile as the problem.

But again, I started decluttering the house before he knew I was on a quest for big change, so I *couldn't* focus on his clutter. I *had* to start by working on mine. I purged my own stuff. I purged neutral stuff.

Our house looked better and felt better and functioned better as I decluttered my own things. And strangely, his piles of pocket clutter didn't get on my nerves as much as they once did. His pile was no longer the straw breaking my own Clutter Camel's back. It was just a small pile, and most of it was closed up in a drawer I didn't use anyway.

But something else happened. The decluttering bug spread. As he saw me get rid of things he never thought I'd purge and as he enjoyed open space in our home, he started purging his own clutter. He started valuing open space over stuff. He started to experience the joy of having less.

Respecting Others with Containers

I had to learn to navigate through Other People's emotions over clutter. By *Other People*, I mean my husband and my kids. The big advantage I have in this area is that I completely understand irrational attachments to physical objects.

I self-analyze my own irrational attachments through blogging. My family doesn't have that luxury, so they may have no idea why the thought of throwing away a certain ratty T-shirt makes them hyperventilate.

Once I personally understood the Container Concept and saw it significantly reduce my own angst when making decluttering decisions, I shared the concept with my family.

I didn't sit them down for a lecture. Instead, I pointed out containers.

To my husband, I said, "I cleaned out that moving-box-we-cover-with-a-tablecloth-and-pretend-is-a-table in our bedroom. You can have it for your high school and college stuff so you'll have room in your closet for all of your clothes."

To my kids, I said, "Put your favorite books on this shelf. Once the shelf is full, we'll get rid of the ones that don't fit."

The Container Concept is simple, and it works. Providing containers (even if that simply means pointing out the limitations of a shelf) does two things. First, it shows them I respect their desire to keep things they deem important. Second, the container is a tangible, visible boundary that determines how much they can keep.

The container imposes limits so I don't have to. The container shows them it makes no sense to keep a waterlogged magazine if keeping that magazine means giving up a treasured book with pages that *don't* stick together. I don't have to be the mean mama.

> The container imposes limits so I don't have to.

Don't Sacrifice the Relationship

I'm putting this chapter at the end of the book. Maybe you read this far, thinking how my words would help someone else in your home. Maybe you really are the world's most organized person, and if it wasn't for the person who lives with you, your home *would* be perfect.

I wrote this book for the person who wants to change, not the person who would like to change someone else. As someone who doesn't like to be told what to do, someone seeking to change me makes me bristle. And I resist.

My messy ways drove my mother crazy when I was growing up. She tried method after strategy after trick to help me change. She motivated. She disciplined.

But she didn't stop loving me or letting me know I was loved. Now that I'm a messy adult, we still have a great relationship.

Go ahead. Encourage, set up routines, declutter. Do whatever you can do to help. But do not, under any circumstance, sacrifice your relationship over this issue.

People are more important than stuff. Period. Always make it clear to the people you love that even though messiness irritates you, you love them more.

If you truly can't get past your frustration, get professional help. Most likely, there's more to the stuff (your irritation with it or your loved one's obsession with it or both) than just stuff.

Proof It's Not Just Me

"The Container Concept finally gave me and my husband a mutually understandable language for discussing how much of something we keep. I love simplicity, emptiness, openness. My husband loves abundance and can think of a million possible uses for everything. We used to be unable to work together.

Me: We don't need all these [items].
Him: But we could use them for [lists dozens of different ideas].
Me: But we don't.
Him: But we might.

It didn't get us anywhere. Here's the new conversation:

Me: Where should we store these?
Him: [Suggests a location.]
Me: Great, do you know someone who needs the ones that don't fit, or should we just donate them?"

—Robin D.

"I am a fairly organized minimalist by nature, living with a disorganized maximalist. We now have two young children, with all the chaos that brings. While I can't advocate getting rid of other people's stuff, I've culled our communal belongings (especially things that are more in my 'territory'—mail, kitchen, clothing, baby gear, household tools). I can't control my partner's desire to keep things, but I can keep the countertops clear."

—Sarah A.

28

Special Circumstances

> **Fantasy:** If only I had more time, more energy, and a bigger house, this would all be easy.

> **Reality:** The life I have is the life I have, and my home is my home. I can't change those things, so I might as well make the best of them.

We're in the last section of the book. Honestly, this section could have the same name as the first: Reality Check. Embracing reality is both the key to getting started and the key to making changes last. *Sorry.*

We've covered it all, right? How to keep a home from being a Disaster Zone on a mostly-daily basis. How to whittle your overabundance of stuff down to a level you can actually manage without losing your mind.

But what if you have special circumstances? What if your life is different than mine?

I receive e-mails from women who have seen huge changes in their homes because they follow the strategies I share. I love these e-mails, but something about them used to confuse me. They often include this phrase: "I relate to you because I _____." And the blanks are filled with all sorts of different things.

Some say they relate to me because they work full time outside the home, but I work from home. Some say they relate to me because they homeschool their children. My kids go to public schools. Some fill in the blank with "suffer from chronic pain" or "have twin babies" or "am single," but none of those things describes me.

But occasionally, I hear the exact opposite from women who haven't tried the strategies yet.

You know the difference? The people for whom these strategies work are the ones who wash their dishes.

The Official Bursting of the Bubble

Here's the thing. There are people in the world with consistently clean homes who suffer from chronic pain, have twin babies, and/or are single. There are people who have consistently clean homes who have ten kids, work three jobs, foster abandoned kittens, and bake banana bread from scratch every Saturday morning.

And there are people who don't work outside the home and have weekly maid service whose homes are consistently a disaster.

I spent years waiting for the next phase of my life to magically improve the state of my home. I had absolutely no doubt whatsoever that *if only* I didn't have such a crazy and unpredictable schedule, or nightly rehearsals after full days of teaching, or such a small apartment, or a house with no proper storage, or kids in diapers, or whatever I was living in the moment, I would be organized.

As each new phase of life unfolded, I was disappointed again to learn my messiness hadn't been magically cured by my circumstances.

Things finally changed when I accepted this: the basics are the basics no matter the unique situation.

A home that doesn't have a system for dealing with the basics will consistently get out of control, no matter how much free time its inhabitants have. A home with systems in place for dealing with the basics can avoid

Disaster Status even if its inhabitants are frazzled and overworked and exhausted.

Don't get me wrong. Cleaning schedules and organizing tricks are not one-size-fits-all, and the struggle is most definitely more real for some than others. And keeping up with the basics *is* more difficult when you're dealing with babies and deadlines and pain. But your life is your life. Your family is the size that it is, and your work schedule and the size of your home may be things you truly can't change.

No matter what your days look like, you need clean dishes and you need clean socks. Comparing your situation to someone else's doesn't change that. Because I have boiled down these home management tasks to the most basic they can be, try them. If they don't work for you in the exact way they do for me, you'll figure out how they do work for you *by trying them*. You won't figure out anything if you talk yourself out of trying.

> A home with systems in place for dealing with the basics can avoid Disaster Status even if its inhabitants are frazzled and overworked and exhausted.

Feeling overwhelmed with your life and schedule can work the same as being overwhelmed with a cluttered space. You don't know where to start. *Do the easy stuff first.*

Instead of being paralyzed by the overall chaos, focus small. Go slowly. Start with the smallest daily tasks that you can't imagine would impact the overall craziness of your life, and let yourself be surprised (even shocked) at the stress that's eliminated by getting things like dishes or bathroom clutter or laundry under control.

But don't get caught up in the crazy notion that there's only one way to make things happen. Accept your unique circumstances, and do what needs to be done. Here are some ideas and mind-set changes I've seen work for various special circumstances.

Moms in High-Stress Work Situations

First, be sure you're not hurting yourself by holding on to principles at the expense of what's practical. You can't do everything. It's not possible. Find the awkward pauses in your days, and fill them with the most basic of basics in order of maximum impact (all of that is in the appendix, "28 Days to Hope for Your Home"). The big picture is overwhelming, but if you chip away at it, basic habit by basic habit, you'll be amazed at the impact.

If you legitimately try and still feel like you're drowning, decide what you can outsource to free brain space and release yourself from the guilt of things that are never going to happen so you can focus on the things that will.

I know. Outsourcing usually involves spending money, so I hesitate to recommend it. I'm frugal. (Frugal to my own detriment sometimes.) This book is written to help you get your home under control without spending more than a few dollars here or there for some basic cleaning products.

If meal planning overwhelms you, even when doing it my way, spend a few dollars to try out a meal-planning service. Search "meal plan with printable grocery list" on the Internet or my website, and you'll find many affordable options. Some can be purchased one week at a time for a few dollars, and some are monthly subscriptions that will deliver recipes and shopping lists via e-mail each week. I subscribed to a meal-planning service for a few years and was amazed at the brain power and energy it freed up in my life. Remove the constant nagging stress of daily meal planning from your already busy schedule, and your overall stress level will go down. You may find that removing this stress gives you more time and energy to keep the basics like dishes and laundry under control in your home.

Now, let's talk about the kind of outsourcing that tends to, strangely, get people fired up. If you've worked on your daily dishwashing routine and are using your five-minute pickup to keep disaster at bay, but you are constantly stressed over the state of your bathrooms or kitchen floors and resent the time spent on these things that you need to spend elsewhere, *you may need to give yourself permission to hire someone to clean your house.* There.

I said it. But pretty please, don't stop reading yet. If you're anything like me, there are two reactions you might have to that statement.

First, fury. "Well, *yeah*. If I could afford a maid, I wouldn't have any of these problems! Any of them. And I definitely wouldn't buy a book about home management written by a self-professed slob!"

Or delight. "Woo-hoo! She said I can hire someone to clean for me! No more dishes or laundry or bending over for me—ever!"

I'll deal with the delusional stuff first. Let me be clear. Having someone clean is awesome, but it does not solve slob problems. Years ago, when I lived overseas, I paid someone to clean my apartment every week. Most cleaners in the United States come once or twice a month. If you never wash your dishes, the cleaner will spend his/her entire time in your home washing your dishes and won't get to other things. Same goes for clutter. If you never put things away, the cleaner won't be able to do what she needs to do.

> Having someone clean is awesome, but it does not solve slob problems.

Basically, the daily stuff is the daily stuff whether you hire cleaning help or not. Work on those things and then, if your lifestyle and budget permit, consider hiring someone to do your bigger, weekly(ish) tasks like cleaning bathrooms and floors, etc.

Even if you're realistic and know this is something that would truly benefit your family, you might not be able to justify the expense. I can't now (though I hope to someday), so I have to manage using the strategies I've shared already. But perhaps, if you're eating at home more often because you're following a meal plan, you could move money from that budget and hire someone to help you clean once each month or even once each season.

You can even outsource laundry. See if local Laundromats offer the service or ask around. Someone you know (or someone *they* know) might want to earn some extra money. Decide what you're willing and able to pay and include that amount in your request. If you're uncomfortable sending your family's unmentionables off to be laundered by someone else, send everything but those.

You have my permission to do whatever needs to be done, realistically, in your real life, in *your* unique home, to get the things done that have to be done.

But here's what you don't have my permission to do. (Not that my permission actually matters.) You don't have my permission to give up and not do anything because you wish you could hire a cleaner.

Ideas for Those with Chronic Pain

Many people who suffer from chronic pain tell me the most difficult adjustment was going from being the person with the sparkly clean home to truly not being able to physically keep their homes up to their own standards. Embracing reality often involves a true grieving process as those with chronic pain accept their new normal.

With chronic pain, energy is limited and unpredictable. Those moments when energy comes are your awkward pauses. Once you understand what the basics are, tackle them in order of maximum impact in your moments of energy so when the energy is gone, you'll see visible progress from your effort.

Also remember that less stuff equals less potential mess, so purge as much and as often as you are able. If you're offered help, direct your helpers to follow these same strategies so you can build upon their work when you are able.

For Those with Very Limited Space

Accept that the Container Concept is a law of nature. Consider me your personal Isaac Newton of decluttering concepts. (Didn't gravity always exist, and every kid knew apples fell straight to the ground? Someone just needed to explain how and why that happens.) Also accept that your home is your home. The home I live in now is many times the size of other spaces I once blamed for my messiness. Yet this is the home that brought me to a point so desperate that I started a blog about it all. It's not about the size of your home; it's about understanding that your home is a container.

For True Hoarders

I'm not going to diagnose or prescribe anything, as I know this is a condition that needs professional help. But I'm talking to those of you who have made it to this point in the book who consider yourselves (or worry that you should consider yourselves) hoarders. You're making progress just by continuing to read and understand.

Do your dishes, even if that takes you all month. Work until you get every single one clean, washing newly dirtied ones within twelve hours of dirtying them. Throw away trash. Keep throwing away trash, even if that's all you can do. If washing dishes and throwing away trash are too overwhelming to consider, even in very small doses, you need to search for a therapist in your area. You've read this book through (maybe even twice), which means you've admitted there's a problem. You're ready.

We all think no one else understands what our lives are actually like, and we're right. We are *all* right. No one understands. But remember this line from one of the first chapters? "Ideas weren't making a difference. The only thing that made a difference was actually doing something. Cleaning with whatever I had on hand, whether it was the perfect thing or not."

Almost two hundred pages later, it's still true.

29

But Will It Last?

Fantasy: I'm serious this time. I've learned from my past mistakes, and I'm finally making changes that will last.

Reality: I am making changes that will last, but they're different changes than I thought they would be.

We're here. The end of this book. The end of the book you started reading because you are overwhelmed in your home.

I will now answer your real question, the one that would probably be your only question if you had to pick just one: Will it last?

Can it last? Can someone who has struggled for years, or even her entire life, conquer her messiness problem?

Yes. But not in the way I once thought.

Once upon a time, I thought I would finish. My house would be under control and stay that way forever. My happily-ever-after was a misty scene of family happiness and smiles with a perfectly clean house in the background.

Over the past seven years of my own deslobification process, my home has changed drastically. More important, though, *I have changed*. The changes in me are the ones that let me answer yes to the "Will it last?" question.

I Have Embraced Reality

I have stopped waiting for the next phase of my life to magically remove my messiness issues. I want to live comfortably in my home with my family . . . *right now*. But rather than simply adopt a positive mantra, I've identified the areas where this mind-set is difficult to maintain, so I notice when a red light flashes brightly and frantically along the tracks of my train of thought.

Living now means living in the home I have. Every time I've ever moved, when I saw the space before I actually lived in it, I envisioned a perfectly decorated and organized home. But soon after settling, I saw there were not enough spaces to stuff all my stuff, and I began dreaming of the next place. I assumed the fault was in the house.

Now I know the truth. I had too much stuff. I now view my home as my family's container. We, plus all of our stuff, need to fit inside it comfortably. The rooms and drawers and closets I have determine how much stuff I can have. I don't have to make that decision, and I love having the weight of that decision removed.

> I refuse to put off having a comfortable home until my kids are gone and I "have time."

I refuse to put off having a comfortable home until my kids are gone and I "have time." I won't have time. I've shattered that delusion about whatever phase is coming next, time and time again. I consciously choose to solve the unique problems in my unique home in this unique phase of life, whatever that means. As long as we can do what we need to do and enjoy one another, I'm succeeding.

I Have Learned from the Best Teacher Ever

I'm so glad you read my book, but I am not your teacher. You need to learn from the teacher who taught me. That teacher's name is Experience.

I read books and asked questions and observed the homes of others, but only when I actually did the dishes every day did I understand how this habit (or nonnegotiable task or daily task or pre-made decision) worked. When I washed my dishes, I saw the impact of washing my dishes. I felt the impact. I experienced the difference this simple task makes in my home when I do it daily.

I understood my own need to have less stuff when I experienced life with less stuff. I moved comfortably through my home. I saw the shockingly positive impact of a five-minute pickup on a home with established places for (almost) everything. I re-decluttered again and again and saw that, with each removal of unnecessary things, necessary things stayed in order a little longer. And as these things happened, I understood my own Clutter Threshold.

My family and I live a lifestyle of decluttering. We always have a donatable Donate Box sitting in our donate spot by the back door. While I will always have decluttering projects, they are fewer and farther between and significantly less overwhelming because we all are willing to throw away broken toys as soon as they break and place clothes in the Donate Box as soon as we realize they are too small. We've experienced less, and we like it.

I have established routines that work in the midst of a crazy life. As I wrote this final chapter, hurtling toward an overwhelming deadline, I stopped. I rose from the chair at my messy kitchen table and moved laundry from my washing machine to my dryer. I divided the huge pile of dark clothing into two smaller (but still substantial) piles of school uniforms and sweaty workout clothes. I started another load.

I can tell you with complete confidence that I would never have stopped a creative project with a looming deadline for something as inconsequential as laundry six years ago. But experience has taught me, has utterly convinced me, has let me learn the hard way that a Laundry Day is worth stopping what I am doing for five to fifteen minutes, six times every Monday. I know from experience that it can be done. When Monday is over, I know from experience I won't have to think about the fullness of my children's sock drawers for the rest of this final week of writing.

I have told you what I have done and the impact these things have had on my home, but now you must experience these things for yourself. I feel your skepticism because I've felt my own. Do your dishes every day for a week whether you have a dishwasher or have to wash by hand. Experience what it means to do the dishes every single day (before they return to Project Status) in your unique home, with your unique schedule and family size and situation, no matter what. That experience will teach you more than I ever can.

If you know in your heart that Laundry Day is the dumbest idea ever written, do a load of laundry every day for a week. At the end of the week, rejoice that you have conquered laundry and know from *experience* how the routine needs to work in your home. If you happen to find out that you share my rewashing-the-same-load-four-days-in-a-row struggles, try Laundry Day for at least three weeks. Experience the third Laundry Day and know for certain whether it works in your home.

Nodding your head in agreement or shaking it in disgust as you read a book or browse the Internet does nothing to improve your home. You are the only one who can improve your home, and you can't know what works until you experience what works.

> You are the only one who can improve your home, and you can't know what works until you experience what works.

Effort is always required to keep a home under control. Others who don't struggle like I do *are* putting forth effort, but their effort is going into the right things. They put effort into daily tasks and regular cleaning schedules. They do not put effort into making decisions about things that need to be done every day. They aren't multiplying the effort required to do the dishes by conducting internal negotiations about whether it's worth their time to do the dishes.

Once I established routines and experienced their amazing effect on my home, once I removed decisions and spent my energy on the most basic of daily tasks, I learned from experience that the work is so much less overwhelming when it is just the work alone, not the work plus internal conflict.

Go. Experience. Wash dishes. Declutter. Your Slob Vision will clear with each routine you establish. Your home will improve with each step you take.

I Have Failed

I started my deslobification process determined to be realistic, but I still hoped perfection could be attained. One day, I wouldn't struggle with these things that seem effortless for others.

I will always struggle. My brain doesn't work the way organized people's brains work. Remember the dirty little secret about most organizing advice? It's written by organized people. I wished my "after" pictures could look like their "before" pictures. Realizing my brain worked differently let me take the advice that worked in my home and not worry about the advice that didn't. As long as I kept trying, working, searching, and eventually finding what did work, I was making progress. I was doing better.

Did you notice the casual mention of my messy kitchen table a few paragraphs ago? Messy tables and cluttered floors happen less often than before I started my deslobification process, but they do happen. When I get consumed with a project (for example, writing a book), my TPAD flares and my Slob Vision relapses, but I don't quit.

According to my pre-deslobification-process standards, I will fail. I do fail. But when I fail, I know what will make the most impact, and I know what to do first to regain traction in my home. Knowing is half the battle, but the rest of the battle is doing the work I know must be done.

As long as I keep going, my failures aren't actual failures. Real failure only happens when I quit. Cleaning and organizing, contrary to how I feel when I visit a Normal Person's home, are not competitive sports. My only responsibility is to myself and my own home and my own family. As long as I do the dishes, I'm winning. As long as I don't throw my hands in the air and declare another method has failed, I'm winning. I keep going, even when I don't see the point. I always see the point once the dishes are done.

Will you fail?

Yes. And no. Go back and read the last paragraph, and read it as yourself.

You'll fail, but as long as you don't quit, you'll succeed.

What's Different Now?

You know what to do, and you are not alone.

I won't blab on about the "you know what to do" part, because you already know to do the dishes.

But the "you are not alone" part is equally important.

Once upon a time, I wanted to write about my strengths. I had no intention of lying, so I planned to talk only about things I did well. I wanted to encourage women in this beautiful journey of family and children and life, and I truly believed sharing the things I'd already mastered was the best way to encourage others.

I was wrong. Years after the acceptance that my practice blog was my real blog, I still despise showing photos of another messy-again space. But I've learned that being completely honest about my struggles provides encouragement to people who desperately need hope.

I'm still Slob Blogging. I'm still sharing "before" pictures of spaces that were once successful "after" pictures. If you head to my blog after finishing this book, you may land on a post that shows a messy-again-for-the-umpteenth-time master bedroom. You may see the results of a pre-made decision justified away in the midst of a busy week.

But look around. You will also find years' worth of day-by-day examples of someone struggling and learning and continuing on no matter what. You will see the moments when my strategies were created out of necessity. You'll read the stories of how I have applied those strategies again and again in my everyday life. You'll see the comments from thousands of other women who relate to my struggles and who understand you.

You've found your people. You aren't alone; you aren't defective. Just keep going. I promised you in the beginning of the book that every strategy in it would be based on experience and proven in reality. That every piece of advice I would share had been thoroughly tested and retested in my personal Slob Lab.

Now it's time for you to learn how this works in your own home.

Step 1: Do the dishes.

. . . .

One Last Proof That It's Not Just Me

"You said you'll always struggle with this. I find that helpful! It means I don't need to strive to 'conquer' this beast, and perfection just isn't going to happen. But struggling? That's something I can identify with! And seeing how far you've come, even though you're still struggling, and seeing how far I've come (I've already done more in the last two weeks than the last two years!) helps so much. I know it sounds like a paradox, but hearing the struggle never ends actually gives me hope."

—Bridget W.

Appendix

....

28 Days to Hope for Your Home

(Not for the Mildly Disorganized)

Develop four habits over four weeks.
Find hope for real change in your home.

Now for the oft-referenced day-by-day guide I promised throughout the book. I know how much more fun it is to read about cleaning than to actually clean, so the purpose of this is to talk you through the next four weeks. Feel free to ignore this appendix and implement every last strategy from the book before you go to bed tonight. But if you're overwhelmed at the thought of actually getting started, just do the assignment for day 1. Keep going tomorrow on day 2, and by the end of the week, I think you'll be amazed at the difference that ridiculously simple tasks done day after day will make in your home.

Day 1

Do the dishes.

That's it. It's not rocket science, so go get started.

And don't worry—you're not alone if doing the dishes means running the dishwasher six times and handwashing every pot and pan in the house because they're *all* dirty. Or even if doing the dishes means you need to run to the store and get dishwashing liquid because you forgot to grab it the last three times you went.

You can do this. So go do it.

See you tomorrow!

Day 2

So, how did it feel having all those dishes clean at once? Strange?

Notice how I used the past tense? I said how "did" it feel because I'll bet some of those dishes you washed are dirty again.

So irritating, right? My family does that too. That it's-time-to-eat-again-and-I-need-to-use-a-fork thing.

Are you ready for your big, life-changing day 2 task?

Do the dishes again.

That's it.

Seriously.

Day 3

Any guesses about today's task?

That's right. **Do the dishes.**

But let's talk for a minute before you do. How long did it take you the first day? How long did it take yesterday? Any difference?

I'm adding one thing to today's task. It's kind of the same thing, but not.

Part 1: Do the dishes right now. Like, as soon as you finish reading this page.

Part 2: Do the dishes before you go to bed.

I know, twice in one day seems like something only a crazy clean freak would do. But you are reading this because you wanted hope. Obviously, the way things are in your home is causing some level of despair.

My gift to you? You don't have to put them away. Just let your hand-washed stuff air-dry and/or leave the clean stuff in the dishwasher until tomorrow morning.

Day 4

You've done the dishes three days in a row! *That* is something about which you can be proud!

Today, you have two tasks. Both involve dishes, but they are done at different times. I'm also going to go ahead and give you a task for tomorrow.

Right now: Go put your dry dishes away from last night.

Tonight: Do the dishes before you go to bed.

Tomorrow morning (as soon as you get up): Put away your dry dishes from tonight.

Day 5

Did you put your dishes away this morning? If so, go look at your kitchen. How does it look compared to how it looked before you started on day 1?

Here's the goal: This dishes-done-kitchen should start to look "normal" to you. I want you to get used to it looking this way. It's not just a special thing that only happens when you throw a party. It's not something you would only see in someone else's home. It's *your* new normal. And when you no longer expect a teetering pile in the sink, moving a single dish won't seem like a pointless task.

And that's today's task. Put single dishes either into the dishwasher or into the sink (if you don't have a dishwasher) as soon as they get dirty. Throughout the day, *as you use a dish*, be conscious about what you do with it.

A big part of changing your home is changing your thoughts. Whatever you automatically did before wasn't working, because it resulted in over-whelming amounts of dishes on the counter and day-long dishwashing marathons.

Putting one dish in the emptied-that-morning dishwasher or into the sink takes about three seconds. Somehow, though, putting thirty dishes in the have-I-emptied-that-yet? dishwasher takes a lot longer than *ninety* seconds.

Just so you know, *we're still on habit one.* This habit is called "doing the dishes." Who knew it was so easy? Who knew it had so many parts?

Put individual dishes in the sink/dishwasher throughout the day today.

Do the dishes tonight.

Put your clean dishes away tomorrow morning!

Day 6

If you started this process on a Monday, today is Saturday. Around here, Saturdays mean *no routine*! Which is wonderful. But if you're tentatively/ desperately trying to begin a new routine, the wonderful freedom that has always been your Saturday may scare you.

If it *isn't* Saturday today, perhaps you are having another kind of out-of-the-routine day or are lamenting the fact that you got behind on day 3. Perhaps you are scared to death that this is going to be one more failed "method."

If that's you, take a deep breath . . . *and do the dishes.* Two days' worth of dishes is easier to do than three days' worth. And three days' worth is *much* easier than a week's worth.

Today, just focus.

Put away your dishes.

Place individual dirty dishes in the sink/dishwasher.

Wash your dishes/start the dishwasher before you go to bed.

Day 7

It's the last day of your first week of hope.

Are you feeling a teensy glimmer yet? If not, it's okay. Just enjoy your clean(er) kitchen, and let it spur you to keep going in week 2.

Since day 7 might be Sunday (and, therefore, might be *another* out-of-the-routine day for you), I want to briefly discuss what can be the biggest frustration in this process.

Other People.

Specifically, Other People who live in your home.

My best advice? Take a deep breath . . . and do the dishes.

As someone who is years farther down the path, I can tell you there *is* hope for them. But right now, this isn't about the Other People in your house; it's about you.

You need to stop worrying over what they are doing or not doing, or what bugs or doesn't bug them, and keep working on changing your habits.

Their change will come down the road. **Don't look for it in week 1.**

So, if you're getting that familiar panicky feeling in your chest, that I-*cannot*-fail-at-this-again feeling, just allow yourself to focus on the dishes.

Put away the clean ones.

Place individual dirty dishes in the sink/dishwasher throughout the day.

Wash the dishes at night.

That second task is the one that might send you over the edge with the Other People in your house. On an out-of-the-routine day, you either have people at home who aren't generally there (and who haven't even *seen* the put-dishes-in-the-dishwasher thing yet), or if you work outside the home, *you* haven't had to do that yet with a full day's worth of dishes. When lots of people are home during the day, there are *more* dishes than when they are gone. It's a fact.

My advice is to have them put their own dishes in the sink/dishwasher *if* you remember to instruct them at the end of the meal. Asking for help to clear the table at the end of a meal is natural and will begin to establish some of *your* new habits as family habits.

If you remember at the moment when your family has just started watching a favorite movie, *do it yourself.* That goes against all good parenting instincts, but remember that you are only seven days into the process of creating habits that will establish an environment in which you can properly train your children in these things.

Day 8

I hope that doing the dishes daily is starting to feel normal to you. Not fun, but normal. As in, your hand automatically knows where to grab the dish-washing liquid, and it's not a three-minute search to find the dish brush. I also hope (and this is my main hope) you are starting to see that doing one day's worth of dishes *isn't* a daunting task.

If you're not, and if three out of the last seven days didn't go as you wanted them to, it's okay. Just keep doing the dishes. Move on to week 2. Each day will include doing the dishes, and if that's all you're able to do . . . then that's all you're able to do.

Put away clean dishes.

Put individual dirty dishes in the sink/dishwasher throughout the day.

I'm going to make an assumption. I'm guessing that because you've had some days when you couldn't believe how quickly you finished the dishes, you did something crazy like wipe down the counters or the kitchen table. If not, that's okay. If so, keep doing that. It's amazing how wiping counters is a natural extension of doing dishes.

Today's new task? **Sweep the kitchen.**

I'm giving you permission to spend an hour or so at this task. The reality for a slob is that sweeping isn't *just* sweeping. It's picking up napkins that got knocked off the table (last month) and the newspapers from (the past few) Sunday(s). It's putting away last week's groceries and getting rid of the bags they were still sitting in. It's gathering up the small and not-so-small toys and knocked-off-the-fridge alphabet magnets.

Once all that is done, you can sweep (after you find the broom).

Tonight, do the dishes before you go to bed.

Day 9

Did your kitchen feel different when you walked into it this morning? With no dishes scattered around and the floor clear, I'm guessing it did.

Today, just do the same thing you did yesterday.

Put clean dishes away in the morning.

Sweep the kitchen.

Place individual dirty dishes in the sink/dishwasher throughout the day.

Do the dishes before you go to bed.

Day 10

Ten whole days of not having to dig around for a clean fork. How does it feel?

Put away the clean dishes.

Sweep the kitchen.

Can you believe how quickly you can sweep the kitchen now that you've done it three days in a row? Can you believe how much dirt and debris accumulates on your kitchen floor in just twenty-four hours?

You've been focusing on your home for ten whole days now. (Even if it's not ten consecutive days!)

The reality is that life rarely goes on for ten days without something happening. When you suddenly realize you haven't even thought about the state of your home (much less about this new do-the-dishes-and-sweep-every-day thing) in two days, just take a deep breath—and do the dishes. While you might feel like you're swimming in Jell-O as you move toward the sink, you'll be amazed at how quickly it will all come back to you.

After the dishes, grab the broom and sweep. Even if it's a middle-of-the-floors-only sweep that takes less than a minute, it will make things easier tomorrow when you're back on track.

Before you go to bed, do the dishes again. I know. That's twice in one day, but the goal is to get back on rhythm.

Day 11

Put away your clean dishes.

Sweep the kitchen.

Put dirty dishes in the sink/dishwasher as they get dirty.

Now that having a nondisastrous kitchen is starting to feel normal, and like something you could maybe really keep up with, you're probably starting to wonder when we're going to get to some real cleaning.

We're not.

The goal of "28 Days to Hope for Your Home" is to guide you to develop four habits that will help you keep your home under control and out of Disaster Status. And contrary to the assumptions of a Slob Brain, day-long cleaning sessions are not what do this. The daily stuff does it.

With that said, go ahead and pick a project. Your day likely feels longer now that you've accomplished so much (a pretty-much-clean kitchen) in a small amount of time. You have permission to use that extra time to bake some cookies with your kids. Or scrub down the bathrooms. Or choose a decluttering project.

If you choose to declutter, follow my Visibility Rule. Choose a small, highly visible space to declutter so you're more likely to complete it before something happens to distract you, and you'll be encouraged every time you walk by it.

Before you go to bed, wash the dishes and wipe down the table/counters.

Day 12

Put away your clean dishes.
 Wipe down the counters/table.
 Sweep the kitchen.

Did you just call me sneaky? Last night, I casually added in wiping down the table and kitchen counters. Casually, because there's a good chance you were already doing this. A quick wipe of the counters with an already-wet dishcloth happens pretty naturally when you're doing the dishes.

Who knew, right?

Before you go to bed, do the dishes. (And wipe down the counters/table.)

Day 13

Is it Saturday? Even if it's not, let's talk about Saturdays again. *The day off.*
I have bad news and good news.

The bad news is that, for a slob, *there's no such thing as a day off.* Really, it's true for every home manager, but Normal People don't see it that way.

We think of putting our dishes in the sink or the dishwasher as work. We view wiping down the counter after making a special lasagna as work.

Normal People don't consider *not* putting their dishes in the sink. They wipe the splatter of marinara off the counter without even thinking about it.

We view that splatter as a personal attack. That splatter is proof this clean-house-thing is impossible. "I've been washing and wiping and even *sweeping* all week long, and now that stupid tomato sauce proves that nothing I do to try to clean this house really matters. None of it lasts!"

Now wipe up that splatter, and let yourself feel foolish over your inner monologue. Did you notice how it took all of three seconds *or less* to wipe it up because it wasn't crusted yet? Did you notice how it was just one splat, not a counter layered with unwiped crusty splatters from the past week?

Put away the clean dishes that you (perhaps) forgot to put away this morning, wipe down the counters and table, sweep the kitchen, and do today's dishes.

Day 14

Put away your clean dishes.
 Sweep the kitchen.

Yes, even if it's Sunday. Another day that's free of routine or at least has a different routine.

You've probably started to grasp the need to make basic, daily tasks part of your normal weekday. You've even accepted that it's necessary to find a way to do these tasks on a day free of routine. But what about the day with a *different* routine? A day with its own unique obligations?

My Sundays involve me leaving for church at 8:15 and my family leaving at 9:00 because I have to be there early for music rehearsal. I try to get my kids' clothes together before I leave. Many times I do this on Saturday night, but sometimes I'm rushing around trying to match shoes and tights and bows, while also getting myself ready. Emptying the dishwasher the moment I get up on Sunday morning rarely enters my mind.

But knowing that emptying the dishwasher is *necessary* helps when I walk into the house on Sunday afternoon and feel the familiar despair over a kitchen that once again looks messy. A kitchen with crusty cinnamon-roll pans and half-full/half-empty cups of milk scattered on the breakfast table.

I know that all I have to do is . . . *wash the dishes*.

Having a list of things that are the bare minimum means that I have a plan. On the days with a different routine, having a list helps.

Do the tasks today *at some point*.

Put away your clean dishes.

Sweep the kitchen.

Put dirty dishes in the sink or dishwasher.

And, before you go to bed, do the dishes.

Day 15

Put away your clean dishes and wipe down the counters/table.

Sweep the kitchen.

Throughout the day, put dirty dishes in the sink/dishwasher as they get dirty.

It's week 3! Are you itching to move beyond the kitchen?

Just a word of warning/wisdom gained from personal experience: it's fine to add extra tasks like toilet-cleaning, vacuuming, or decluttering—as long as you've already done the daily tasks.

We slobs love big projects. We're generally creative people who love to get consumed with something that will finish with a wow factor. Unfortunately, there's not much of a wow factor in washing the dishes. But remember: the little things are more important than the big things. Not *just as* important, but *more* important.

So what's the new little thing for this week? **Check the bathrooms for clutter.**

Yeehaw! We're moving beyond the kitchen! Not past it, because it's still number one on the must-do-every-single-day list. But once you've done your kitchen tasks for the day, take a walk through the house, consciously looking into every bathroom. For today, ignore the ring around the bathtub. Ignore the smell. Just deal with the clutter.

The dirty undies and the magazines strewn across the floor. The damp towels and the empty toilet paper rolls. Pick up those things and put them where they should go. Wring out the six used washcloths that are sitting in the bottom of the shower, and throw them in the washing machine. Straighten the wadded-up rug, and close the shower curtain.

Now clear the counter. Put the toothbrushes where they go, cap the toothpaste, take the Pool Partyin' Barbies to their owner's room.

You likely can't resist wiping down the counters at this point. Go ahead, but remember this task is about the clutter.

Before you leave for the next bathroom, step out and then step back in. Is the difference noticeable?

Before you go to bed tonight, do the dishes and wipe down the counters/table.

Day 16

Put away your clean dishes and wipe down the counters/table.

Sweep the kitchen.

Check the bathrooms for clutter.

Throughout the day, put dirty dishes in the sink/dishwasher as they get dirty.

Glance in each bathroom. Are you amazed they look pretty good? Compared to yesterday, it's like they're *clean*! I mean, *one* little piece of clothing on the floor . . . that hardly bothers you! And a toothbrush haphazardly left on the counter? What's the big deal?

Just pick up the clothes and put the toothbrush back where it goes.

Before you go to bed, do the dishes.

Day 17

Put away your clean dishes and wipe the counters/table.
  Sweep the kitchen.
  Check the bathrooms for clutter.
  Put dirty dishes in the sink/dishwasher as they get dirty.
  Seriously? *More* dirty clothes on the floor?

Didn't your family members notice this bathroom has looked ten times better for the past two days? Did it *not* occur to them that *their* pair of dirty socks was the only thing marring the otherwise clear-for-once floor?

Take a deep breath.

If they're not home right now, pick up the socks yourself. But if they are home, call them into the bathroom and show them their socks. Have them pick up the socks and ask them to start doing this daily. In-the-moment parenting is always most effective. Don't get annoyed when they look like they don't recognize you. Remember what the bathroom looked like on day 15? *That's what they think a bathroom is supposed to look like.* They think you're okay with that because you were.

Until two days ago.

Mad that I'm suggesting you not leave those socks on the floor so you can make your point when the kids get home? Let's be honest here. There's a decent chance you'll forget to tell your kids to pick them up tonight . . . and then you'll have two days' worth of clothes on the floor tomorrow.

Tonight, before you go to bed . . . wash the dishes.

Day 18

Put away your clean dishes.
  Sweep the kitchen.

Put dirty dishes in the sink/dishwasher.
Check the bathrooms for clutter.

Have you rebelled yet?

Let's talk about it. Over the next few days, I'm going to talk about different reasons you may be rebelling. (If you're not rebelling yet, you're a better person than I am.)

You don't have the time. Seriously, you have *x* number of kids. A full-time job outside the home. Or responsibilities at church. Or kids with allergies whose food has to be made from scratch. Or just better things (or at least more interesting things) to do than clean.

Things come up, and you may truly have days when you do not have time to put away your clean dishes when you get up in the morning. But I'll bet since you've put them away eighteen times in eighteen days, you're getting fairly good at it. You're learning that if you hang a coffee cup on each finger, you can put them all away with only one trip to the coffee-cup cabinet.

Here's the thing the rebellious Slob Brain doesn't want to accept: doing these things daily means you are doing them little by little, which saves time.

Just remember why you started reading this guide. You wanted hope for your home. Unfortunately, hope *isn't* as ambiguous as it sounds. It isn't something that floats around in the sky until it settles on top of your head. It's something you work for. It's something you discover *after* you put in some work.

And really, that's *not* unfortunate. Unfortunate things are out of your control. *This is in your control.*

Now go do the dishes and wipe down the counters and table before you go to bed.

Day 19

Put away your clean dishes.
Sweep the kitchen.

Check the bathrooms for clutter.

Put dirty dishes in the sink/dishwasher as they get dirty.

Still rebelling? Feeling a little smug because yesterday's "address the rebellion" speech wasn't talking about you?

How about this? *I* don't get it. *I* don't get your life. I have only three children and didn't start my deslobification process until two of my three kids were in school. I don't have a "real" job. Blogger? Writer? What*ever*.

Maybe your husband is mean. Maybe your kids are teenagers and have actually laughed out loud at your attempts to change the way things have been for their entire lives. Maybe you're a single mom and work three jobs and still can't pay the bills. Maybe your mother-in-law lives next door and shows up unannounced and says rude things in front of your children. Maybe you have septuplets. Maybe you homeschool. Maybe you don't have a dishwasher or even a double sink.

Maybe you have to wash your clothes by beating them on rocks in the river.

I don't know what your unique situation is, and I don't pretend everyone's life is like mine. But I do know these four habits are as basic as they get.

Doing the dishes is just something that has to be done, even if "doing the dishes" means throwing away the pizza boxes and paper-towels-used-as-plates.

Sweeping the kitchen? Like I said on day 8, it's not about sweeping the kitchen. It's about paying attention to the floor and keeping your kitchen in a state where you can do what needs to be done in it. Without tripping.

Checking the bathrooms for clutter? It's visual. It's paying attention. And if you've really been doing it, there might have been a day or two when *looking* into the bathroom was *all you had to do.*

These things are the basics, the bare minimum. If you want hope, you're going to have to accept that. They are not things you put off until Saturday. They're things that need to be done every day. In every home.

I know. It sucks.

Now go do the dishes.

Day 20

We're in the twenties! And there are only twenty-eight days! (Well, twenty-eight days of this guide. There are, like, a *million* days after that.)

Put away your clean dishes.

Put dirty dishes in the sink or the dishwasher.

Sweep the kitchen.

Check the bathrooms for clutter.

Is it Saturday? Okay then. Go have some fun.

Just do the dishes before you go to bed.

Day 21

What? It's 3:00 p.m. on Sunday, and you haven't done a thing? Oh. You just read the "go have some fun" part of yesterday and ignored the rest?

It's okay.

Do the dishes.

Sweep the kitchen.

Check the bathrooms for clutter.

Do the dishes again before you go to bed.

(Tomorrow starts the final week! Are you excited?)

Day 22

It's the first day of the last week. Have you noticed a change in your home? Have you done some extra decluttering projects with all your freed-up time? Are you feeling the difference? Has anyone noticed?

Put away your clean dishes.

Sweep the kitchen.

Check the bathrooms for clutter.

Do a five-minute pickup.

Oh, yeah. That's the new habit for this week. You've made real change in your kitchen, and the kitchen being clean makes the whole house feel cleaner, right? The bathrooms being clutter-free feels great every time you . . . well . . . *you know*.

But what about the rest of the house? Maybe there aren't any dirty undies on the bathroom floor, but you're tripping over stuff as you walk through the living room.

Take five minutes to pick things up. Oh, and put them away too. All within the five minutes.

For the dishes, the kitchen floors, and the bathrooms, the first day took extra time. Not today. Just five minutes is all you need. Those tasks were specific and involved defined areas. "Picking up the house" is a little more ambiguous. Asking you to do it all today would be a sure way to cause tears of frustration and possibly some ripped-out book pages.

Look at the clock, or set a timer, and spend five minutes picking up. Personally, I would start in the most lived-in room. For us, that's the living room.

Because it's your first day for this habit, you may need to start with a trash bag. Just pick up trash for five minutes.

Tonight, do the dishes before you go to bed.

Day 23

Put away your clean dishes.
   Put dirty dishes in the sink/dishwasher as they get dirty.
   Sweep the kitchen.
   Check the bathrooms for clutter.
   Do a five-minute pickup.
   Do you need to use the trash bag again? If not, you could try spending five minutes gathering things that need to be donated. Bag them or box them up as you go, and then go put them in your trunk at the end of the five minutes.

   Tonight . . . do your dishes and wipe down the counters and table.

Day 24

Put away your clean dishes.
  Place dirty dishes in the sink/dishwasher throughout the day.
  Sweep the kitchen.
  Check the bathrooms for clutter.
  Do a five-minute pickup.

Are you a little amazed at the difference you see from just three days of five-minute pickups? *Just fifteen minutes total?*

Oh. You're amazed. But you don't want to admit it because you're feeling rebellious again.

You're thinking, *Look, lady, all this bathroom-checking and dish-doing and kitchen-sweeping is great, but my shower has a glass door I haven't seen through in three years because the soap scum is so thick! When am I going to clean the bathrooms? Huh?*

Well, I'll go ahead and answer that: whenever you want to.

How about now? Right after you do the dishes, sweep the kitchen, check the bathrooms for clutter, and do a five-minute pickup.

This is why I resisted writing this much-requested deslobification manual for so long. People want a step-by-step guide to having the home of their dreams. But the problem with dreams is that you wake up. And drop your clothes on the bathroom floor. And use forks.

Clean the bathroom. Maybe that can be your big weekly project in place of doing a week's worth of dishes. Y'know, since you don't have to do a week's worth of dishes anymore.

In my home, I have assigned a major cleaning task to each day of the week. I do laundry on Mondays, mop the kitchen on Thursdays, etc. But I didn't start doing that until six months into my deslobification process. During those first six months, I randomly cleaned bathrooms or vacuumed. Yet my home was in better shape than it had ever been.

And I had hope. I saw, through personal understanding and experience-based knowledge, that small, daily habits are the key.

Now go do your dishes and wipe down the counters and table before you go to bed.

Day 25

Put away your clean dishes.
    Place dirty dishes in the sink or dishwasher throughout the day.
    Sweep the kitchen.
    Check the bathrooms for clutter.
    Do a five-minute pickup.
    You've been doing five-minute pickups for five days now. Maybe, today, you'll get through the obvious stuff in the first two minutes. You may be tempted to stand in the middle of the room with a bewildered look on your face for the last three.

If you find yourself standing there, shake your head and focus on something that bugs you. Let's not pretend you're at the point where you need to start analyzing the aesthetic value of the figurines on your fireplace mantel. Look for the things that have escaped your vision. Perhaps it's the love seat covered in clean, unfolded laundry. Perhaps it's the pile of paper on the coffee table. I call this stuff *procrasticlutter*.

Spend any remaining minutes on those things. Fold clothes until the five minutes are *almost* up, and then go put those clothes away. Like, in their drawers and everything.

Or go through coffee table papers looking for things you can trash.
    Tonight, wash the dishes and wipe the counters and table.

Day 26

Put away your clean dishes.
    Place dishes in the sink or dishwasher as they get dirty throughout the day.
    Sweep the kitchen.
    Check the bathrooms for clutter.
    Do a five-minute pickup.
    If you, again, find yourself with three whole minutes left after you've picked up the from-yesterday-to-today stuff in your living room, go back

to whatever you started tackling yesterday. Keep folding laundry. Just leave enough time to put it away before the five minutes are gone. Who knows? You might even find yourself on a roll and end up clearing it *all* off the couch.

Just be ready to comfort your frightened children tomorrow morning when they discover all the clean clothes have disappeared. And to direct them to those things called "dresser drawers."

Speaking of your family, I'm going to ask: has anyone in your family noticed? If they have . . . *yay!* If they haven't, I'm soooo sorry. I feel your pain, and I (far away in my Texas home) understand what a big deal it is that you've made it to day 26.

I know that the discouragement you feel is real. When no one takes your efforts to change seriously (not even your *success* in those efforts), you want to give up.

Just don't let the discouragement win. Keep going. Keep washing the dishes every night, and keep checking your bathrooms for clutter. Enjoy how much easier it is to live in your home. Gain your encouragement from watching your family enjoy it, too, even if they don't realize what they're enjoying.

And if life happens and you prove their theory that this new *method* won't work, just start back on day 1. Because now you know hope is attainable. It just takes work.

Now go do your dishes and wipe the counters and table.

Day 27

Put away your clean dishes.
Place dirty ones in the sink or dishwasher.
Sweep the kitchen.
Check the bathrooms for clutter.
Do a five-minute pickup.

Are you irritated at spending those five minutes picking up everyone else's stuff? If you're doing this while everyone is at home with you, the five-minute pickup is an excellent habit to turn into a group task.

If you're home alone, let your slowly-becoming-less-cluttered space be the reminder to have them do another pickup when they're home.

Really? Two pickups? Why not just wait until we can do one, but all together?

Waiting doesn't work. It may sound noble, like you're exercising patience . . . but let's call it what it really is. Procrastinating.

Just do it. Put their stuff right inside the door to their room. The big clean-out-the-kids'-rooms project isn't even on your radar yet. When they complain, you'll remember to tell them you'd like them to put their *own* stuff away.

See? A win-win.

Before you go to bed tonight, do the dishes. Wipe down the counters and the table.

Day 28

Put away your clean dishes.
Place dirty ones in the sink or dishwasher.
Sweep the kitchen.
Check the bathrooms for clutter.
Do a five-minute pickup.

Woo-hoo! You're done! You've made it to the twenty-eighth day!

Well . . . except for washing the dishes tonight. Oh, and then putting them away first thing tomorrow. And sweeping the kitchen, checking the bathrooms for clutter, and doing your five-minute pickup, of course.

The hope doesn't come from what your house looks like after twenty-eight days. It comes from knowing what it takes to keep it looking that way every day.

Did I just pop your metaphorical balloon?

Sorry.

When I started my blog, I truly believed the project was temporary. I just *knew* if I put my mind to it, I'd kick this chronic-messiness thing, draft a final post called "The End," and spend the rest of my days writing about *much* more interesting things than *cleaning* . . . in my always-orderly home.

That vision has changed. Partly because it's no longer a dream, but reality. Which is both good and bad. The bad part is I've realized there is no magic fix. No end to the dishes or the sweeping or the picking up.

The good news is these are skills. Skills can be learned and honed and practiced and developed. And when they get rusty from lack of use, they can be relearned.

And there's more good news! If you've grown accustomed to hearing my voice in your head every day for the past four weeks, that doesn't have to end. You can go over to http://www.aslobcomesclean.com/manage and read about the real-life daily progress of a real-life slob.

Just know you might land there on a day when I'm feeling like a failure and my kitchen stove is crusty with marinara sauce. Because those days happen.

But now I know . . . to go do the dishes.

* * *

Now that you've finished reading, go get started on day 1.

What? You thought I didn't know you were going to read the whole thing before you washed your first dish? I knew.

Now go do the dishes.

Acknowledgments

I am so incredibly thankful for the people who supported this crazy, heart-wrenching, difficult, and fun book-writing process.

My hot and hilarious husband, Bob: Thanks for making me laugh and for laughing at me. Thanks for living your everyday life inside my Slob Lab and loving me anyway.

My kids, Jackson, Reid, and Presley: Thanks for being excited about this book and all the crazy things I do, even though it's a book about cleaning. Y'all make life fun and meaningful at the same time.

My mom and dad, Peggy and George: Thanks for your unfailing encouragement and support, for lending your lake house as a place to dive into uninterrupted writing time, for helping out with everyday life, for being willing to be my first readers, and for giving me permission to psychoanalyze you publicly whenever I feel like it.

My agent, Jessica Kirkland: Thanks for getting excited about my message of hope and my unique perspective and having the nerve to pitch me to anyone who will listen.

My blog readers/kindred spirits: Thanks for surprising me with the news that I'm not the only one out there who sees the world this way and for convincing me I had something of value to share.

My blog assistant, Linda Sears: Thanks for cheering me on, for taking so much off my plate, and for keeping the blog running while I wrote this book.

My mastermind pals: Thanks for helping me brainstorm, keep focus, and stay sane.

Acknowledgments

My acquisitions editor, Debbie Wickwire: Thanks for seeing the potential in me and in my message and for your desire to spread the word that there's hope for slobs!

My editor, Meaghan Porter: Thanks for your editing wisdom, your excitement over this project, and your encouragement through this process.

Thomas Nelson team: Thanks for your creativity and expertise in making this all happen!

Kim Robbins Photography: Thanks for one of the most fun days of my life, spent making funny faces for the camera in your studio!

My guinea pig reader, Alea Milham: Thanks for offering and taking the time to read my not-yet-edited first manuscript. Your raving encouragement let me sleep peacefully in those final days before turning it in.

God: Thanks for creating me exactly as I am and for directing me on this journey I would never have chosen, but which is so much better than the one I'd have designed.

About the Author

DANA K. WHITE is a blogger, speaker, and (much to her own surprise) Decluttering Expert. She taught both English and Theatre Arts before leaving her job to make her family her life's work. In an attempt to get her home under control, Dana started blogging as Nony (short for Anonymous) at *A Slob Comes Clean*. She soon realized she was not alone in her housekeeping struggles and in her feelings of shame. Today, Dana shares realistic home management strategies and a message of hope for the hopelessly messy through her blog, weekly podcasts, and videos. Dana lives with her husband and three kids just outside of Dallas, Texas. Oh, and she's funny.

Connect with Dana and join a community of
people who are learning to manage their homes
without losing their minds at
http://www.aslobcomesclean.com/manage.